Young People at the Centre

Participation and Social Change

Edited by

Jane Foster and Kumi Naidoo

COMMONWEALTH SECRETARIAT

Commonwealth Secretariat
Marlborough House
Pall Mall
London SW1Y 5HX
United Kingdom

Published by the Commonwealth Secretariat.
Designed by Wayzgoose
Printed in the United Kingdom by Formara
Wherever possible, the Commonwealth Secretariat uses paper
sourced from sustainable forests or from sources that minimise a
destructive impact on the environment.

Copies of this publication can be ordered direct from:
The Publications Manager,
Information and Public Affairs Division,
Commonwealth Secretariat,
Marlborough House,
Pall Mall, London SW1Y 5HX,
United Kingdom
Tel: +44 (0)20 7747 6342
Fax: +44 (0)20 7839 9081
E-mail: r.jones-parry@commonwealth.int

Price: £10.99
ISBN: 0-85092-681-5

Web sites:
www.thecommonwealth.org
www.cypyouth.org

Contents

Commonwealth Youth Programme

Commonwealth Heads of Government established the Commonwealth Youth Programme (CYP) in 1974. Part of the Commonwealth Secretariat based in London, the CYP has regional centres for Africa, based in Zambia; for Asia, in India; for the Caribbean, in Guyana; and for the South Pacific, in Solomon Islands. CYP works with governments and young people's networks for a world where young women and men (aged 15–29 years) can reach their full potential. Commonwealth countries agreed that young people are themselves the best 'resource' for their development, and that young people should be able to 'act on their own behalf, and on their own terms, rather than at the direction of others'.

CIVICUS

CIVICUS is an international alliance dedicated to strengthening citizen action and civil society throughout the world. The organisation's vision is a worldwide community of informed, inspired, committed citizens who are actively engaged in confronting the challenges facing humanity. CIVICUS's members include more than 600 non-governmental organisations, associations, private and corporate foundations, and individuals from over 100 countries. Through its various programmes and projects, CIVICUS aims to heighten awareness among the public and governments on the vital role of civil society in building democracy, promoting gender equality, fostering justice, promoting social inclusion and fighting poverty.

Foreword

Rt. Hon. Don McKinnon, Commonwealth Secretary-General

Most of the world is young. The rest of us have all been young. But it is easy to forget that we are young in a particular social setting. In the developed world, education systems and other institutions may treat youth as a rehearsal for 'real' life. In the developing world, adult responsibilities can come only too soon, leaving hardly a space for childhood. But despite the contrast, something usually lacking in both scenarios is *control* over one's life; a chance to really contribute to the decision-making that affects us. This escapes our attention because we're more likely to think of youth as part of the life cycle, than youth as a social grouping. The advice we give, even to ourselves, is too often: 'wait until you're grown up.'

Postponing young people's participation in this way can be very destructive. In economic terms, it represents a waste of human resources. The loss is more serious now than ever before; social and economic changes today promise benefits that can only be realised through and with young people. Failing that challenge promises grave costs. As this book shows, the alternative to youth empowerment is not the status quo but something far worse. HIV/AIDS is dismantling decades of progress on living standards and life expectancy, decades of development and centuries of cultural memory. Our environment is under threat. Unemployment is rife. This is not a time to sit on our hands. Young people are either part of the effort, or the effort fails.

The Commonwealth Plan of Action on Youth Empowerment, endorsed by Heads of Government in 1999, states that young people are themselves the best resource for their development.

Wherever I go in the Commonwealth, I find this confirmed: young people have strong, constructive views about the development of their communities. I am also impressed by their ability to forge international networks of knowledge and opinion through information technology – again, a theme borne out in this book. So the talent and energy is there to be mobilised. Let's all of us in government, NGOs and the wider community 'think globally and act locally' on youth participation. There are plenty of examples here worth emulating.

Don McKinnon
Commonwealth Secretary-General
London, UK

We are currently witnessing a change in the status of young people – from being mere recipients of adult-led programmes to being active decision-makers. But while many organisations want to be part of this change, they do not know how. This book therefore could not have come at a better time.

I do not believe the decision to involve the young can be postponed. In Africa, HIV/AIDS is succeeding where malaria, slavery and civil strife have failed – it is threatening a continent of young people. Perhaps the question to older generations is: what do you plan to do without us?

Mulako Mwanamwalye (Zambia)
Chairperson, Commonwealth Youth Caucus

Introduction

IN EARLY 1999 CIVICUS, the global alliance for citizen action, together with the Commonwealth Youth Programme (CYP), brought together an ad hoc group of individuals and agencies working with young people. The intention was to create a forum for advocacy and action to engage young people in civil society and social change. The organisations involved included: World Association of Girls Guides and Girl Scouts (WAGGGS), International Youth Foundation (IYF), Development Education for Youth (DEFY), International Business Students Exchange (AIESEC), Commonwealth Youth Programme, Raleigh International and World Organisation of the Scout Movement (WOSM).

Partners for Youth Participation (PYP), as the group calls itself, first acted together at the CIVICUS World Assembly held in Manila, Philippines in 1999. PYP held a series of workshops and breakout groups during the assembly on the theme of youth participation. The workshops were very well attended. A wide range of agencies, individuals and organisations showed interest in the experiences of young people and the benefits that their participation had brought to civil society. There was a real demand for information on *how* to stimulate and institutionalise genuine participation.

At the conclusion of the assembly PYP members agreed that experiences of successful participation needed to be documented. This publication was born out of the need for a simple demonstration of the links between personal empowerment and enabling environments for participation. The aim is to demonstrate the potential of young people, and to enable them and their advocates to speak; to share their experiences and vision of a world in which young people are equal partners.

The methodology for the publication was both framed and constrained by the PYP network. As most of the members of PYP are NGOs with headquarters based across North America and Europe, resources were a critical factor. PYP agreed that we would use our networks and in-house capacity to produce the book. The outline of the publication was agreed at a meeting in London in June 2000. Jane Foster (CYP) and Kumi Naidoo (CIVICUS) became co-editors. Charlotte Barran (WAGGGS), Steve Mokwena (formerly with IYF), Indira Ravindran, Laila Duggan (CIVICUS) and Andrew Robertson (CYP) all made substantial contributions. The range of case studies collected reflects the networks and resources that collectively we have been able to call upon.

In 2001 major international events with a focus on young people will take place. This made the timing of the book critical. Publication was planned so that it could be launched at the CIVICUS World Assembly to be held in Vancouver, Canada, 19–23 August. This will be followed by:

- The UN World Youth Forum 5th session, at which hundreds of youth NGOs and youth civil society groups meet in dialogue with the UN system agencies, August 2001, Dakar, Senegal;

- UN General Assembly Special Session on Children and Adolescents, 'The Future Global Agenda for Children', September 2001, UN, New York;

- Commonwealth Heads of Government Meeting, to be held in Brisbane, Australia, in October 2001. This will consider a new role for the Commonwealth. Engaging young people is already high on the Commonwealth's agenda and the Third NGO Commonwealth Youth Forum will take place at the same time as the Heads of Government Meeting.

So, with great enthusiasm, limited resources and tight deadlines the project commenced in December 2000.

Jane Foster   **Kumi Naidoo**
June 2001, London, UK

Chapter 1

Framing Youth Participation in the Twenty-first Century or 'Missing the Wood for the Trees'

Jane Foster

My friends, no-one is born a good citizen; no nation is born a democracy. Rather, both are processes that continue to evolve over a lifetime. Young people must be included from birth. A society that cuts itself off from its youth severs its lifeline; it is condemned to bleed to death.

Kofi Annan, UN Secretary-General
(UN World Conference of Ministers for Youth, Lisbon, August, 1998)

With adult prevalence rates of around 20 per cent and 35 per cent respectively, South Africa and Botswana are already feeling the impact of the epidemic. Worse is yet to come in both countries, today's 15 year olds have a greater than 50per cent chance of dying of HIV-related causes if the current infection rates are not cut dramatically.

(UNAIDS AIDS epidemic update: December 2000)

There always have been and always will be exceptional young people in the world. Are there really no modern day equivalents to Goliath-slaying Davids or Joan of Arc? At age 12, Canadian Craig Keiggleburger started a campaign against child labour in the sportswear industry that contributed to starting a global movement. Now governments across the world are signing the UN Convention on the Abolition of Child Labour. During the 1980s, Rigoberta Menchu fled her homeland, Guatemala, after the murder of her immediate family. From the age of 22 she worked at home and abroad to secure and protect the rights of indigenous peoples and promote intercultural peace. She was awarded a Nobel Peace Prize for her work in 1992 when she was only 33.

Stark contrasts are facing young people today: on the one hand global commitment to democracy and an increasing demand for active citizenry. On the other, death for more than 50 per cent of today's 15-year-olds in two countries because not enough was done to combat HIV/AIDS by the previous generation. This is an extreme case. But other developments also bode ill for youth participation in conventional politics: the demise of youth sections of political parties, the ageing nature of the Bush administration, the demonising of South African youth who went from being the young lions to the lost generation in five short years.

Young people are not treated as a high priority. They can be, and are being marginalised. In recent national elections in the USA (2000) and UK (2001) there was a low turnout amongst many different ages and sectors of the electorate – but young people were among those least likely to vote.

But as we ask 'who' young people are today – what they are doing or not doing – the first point to note is that they are far from homogeneous. Take the most fundamental level of analysis – demographics. In the developed world the young are dwindling in numbers as the population ages; there is good reason why politicians are increasingly courting the 'grey' vote. But in the South the situation is very different. In some countries up to 70 per cent of the population is less than 30 years of age. There is a huge cohort of young people leaving education in various states of unpreparedness, without access to further training in skills, or even finance for micro-enterprise.

International Labour Organisation (ILO) estimates show the following figures for youth population and entry into the labour force over the next decade:

Global population	6 billion
Aged 15–24	1 billion
Aged under 20	2.4 billion
Entry to labour force, 2000–2010	700 million

These figures should prompt politicians and policy-makers at national, regional and international levels to ask the following kinds of questions:

- Is there a clear relationship between development planning and demography in policy and practice?

- Are positive interventions planned to reflect these demographic trends in education, training, employment and economic activities?

- What would be the positive measurable outcomes of successfully engaging even a fraction of these young people in economic activity?

- What is the worst possible scenario if the labour market entrants – 700 million young people – remain marginalised, excluded and powerless?

New Forms of Participation

In important respects, this is a picture of under-participation. But deeper inspection reveals a more complex set of needs that require new methods to make participation attractive and meaningful. And before we conclude that the young do not participate, we should be careful not to restrict our attention to the most familiar indicators.

Recent research from North America describes the positive environment that nurtures participation, the 'triggers' for civic engagement and the importance of mentors and peer support. A One World (USA) report describes how young activists' 'careers' follow a similar trajectory:

> youth activists [take] lead roles in environmental or justice-based campaigns. They report not only supportive parents and high academic accomplishment, but a precocious development of social consciousness and the early onset of an intense and dogged curiosity about how the world works.

These findings are reinforced by a Canadian study, Social Vision – Young Adult Perspectives on Social and Civic Responsibility by D-Code Inc. and the Canadian Centre for Social Entrepreneurship (April 2001).

> A student active in environmental issues recalls having 'deep feelings of needing to make a change' from the time she was a child but [having been] uncertain how to do it. She was encouraged by a high school teacher who connected her with other youth who felt the same way on issues about the impact of globalisation … she found mentors and fellow young activists who encouraged and inspired her with their commitment and passion, providing her with an outlet for action and expression.

During the period of 'youth' (defined by the UN/Commonwealth as life between the ages of 15 and 30) people experience much change and transition on the way to 'adulthood'. This is an exhilarating challenge. Increasingly it is being observed that precisely because they are in times of personal transition, young people are better equipped than other generational cohorts to embrace changes associated with globalisation.

In a paper on Youth Development and Population (UN ECLAC 2000), youth is described as being at a paradoxical crossroads.

> Modern times are clearly marked by the institutionalisation of change and the centrality of knowledge as the motor of progress. Both factors place young people in a privileged position for contributing to development. But while the realisation of current development styles requires optimal utilisation of the types of assets that are concentrated among young youth, it paradoxically increases social exclusion among young people.

Technology provides a good example of the strengths of the young. In 1986 I was managing youth work in Sheffield in the UK. At a young mothers drop-in centre there were some very basic computers (remember Commodores?). A little girl of three or four drew a flower with a simple draw tool and was filling the petals in with different colours. She was showing no fear of technology, just acceptance of it – as I had accepted crayons 30 years earlier. This spurred me into buying my first PC. I still wonder if that girl (now a young woman) uses IT with the same ease she did at four.

Young people are embracing new forms of activism in both the North and South. They are using their cell phones to text messages to each other to overthrow corrupt politicians (Philippines, January 2001). They are using websites and free e-mail services to create and develop global networks with each other on issues they care passionately about, such as the anti-globalisation protests in 1999–2001. They are communicating and acting in C21st mode. A generational and digital divide is giving young people an edge in organising. In 2000, all members of CYP's youth network in the Caribbean region had personal (often free) e-mail addresses – unlike the national Ministries responsible for Youth Affairs.

Defined, Excluded and Under-Invested

Western notions of childhood, adolescence and transition to adulthood today determine the conceptualisation of young people in the world. Entire industries of physiological and psychological development have grown up around them. (Just look at some headlines from websites/newspapers on youth today.) This concept-ualisation of children and young people is all-pervasive, having been exported to the developing world. 'School dropouts' is a common expression – but in the South it is more likely they didn't get into the education system at all, or were pushed out by the lack of places in secondary education. In the Caribbean I have heard street children disparaged by adults in the education profession – in a country where compulsory secondary education is not available. Where else do young people go after they have failed (or been failed) in the formal education system, where there is little post-primary vocational training?

Whilst training youth development workers in Aotearoa, New Zealand I found a common complaint was 'feeling like the ambulance at the bottom of the cliff'. They were waiting for young people to present as problems, as victims or deviants. The role youth development workers were ascribed was rescue, patching up or 'fixing' young people. Convincing the 'caring professions' to work with and along-side young people to build fences at the top of the cliff was regarded as pretty radical. Youth suicide, drug and alcohol abuse, juvenile crime and teen pregnancy are associated with 'medical' models of intervention. Something is wrong or faulty – it needs to be fixed. Sadly, programme funding, resources for research, training and conferences for adult 'professionals' are often easier to secure than those for young people who can do it for themselves.

In Uganda there is a decentralised system of government. Within this system there are seats exclusively reserved for young people at village, regional and national levels. The elections for these seats are fiercely contested; young people take their participation in democracy and representation very seriously. But there was no written record of this bold engagement of young people by the Museveni government until 2001 (see 'Addressing the Democratic Deficit' – due for publication by the Carnegie Young People's Initiative, late 2001). No-one thought it worth studying, documenting and publishing. There is little literature relating to young people that does not focus on their perceived vulnerability and shortcomings. The image of carefree, irresponsible youth with an appetite and aptitude for sex, drugs and rock and roll is a poor substitute.

There remain large numbers of young people who are under-invested in, particularly those who are out of school for the range of reasons cited earlier. Once these young people part company from child health care or rudimentary basic education, they have little contact with the resources or benefits of investment. Civil society, governmental agencies and international development organisations do not see young people, especially those in the second decade of life (11–20), as a priority.

Programmes targeted at this group of young people are often tackling symptoms that adult society sees as undesirable, with programmes and activities that adult society thinks appropriate for them. Such programmes are designed and imple- mented with little or no consultation with the target beneficiaries. Their impact is greatly diminished for two reasons. Firstly, because they do not engage young people as partners. Doing so would add to young people's insights into their own needs and interests. Secondly, programmes would have a much greater impact if they involved the energy and creativity of the young people themselves.

If we dig deeper behind these Western concepts we can find another reality, one in which young people can and do play important and active roles in family, community, economic life, and political and social change. This is largely undocumented and disregarded. The lack of the body of knowledge means young people lose the history of success and are unable to transmit these important lessons to the next cohort.

The fight against HIV/AIDS gives us an even starker example. From Uganda, Zambia, Thailand, Senegal and, most recently, South Africa, comes good news. Lower infection rates among young people aged 15–19 have been reported. 'Great', you might think, let's find out exactly what caused attitude and behaviour change amongst these young people. But if you scour the websites and literature that pro- liferate on HIV/AIDS you will find it difficult, if not impossible, to find explana- tions for this. The 2000 Durban AIDS conference had plenty of presentations and information about research on drug therapies. But what about identifying the successful interventions that actually result in fewer young people becoming infected? Where is the research? It simply does not exist; young people are not regarded as sufficiently high priority to warrant this investment.

This is despite the fact that health, along with education, is one of the few areas even thought of as demanding investment in young people. Great strides in the well-being of children in the first decade of life (1–10) took place during the early 1990s. However, in the developing world much of this has been, or is in grave danger of, being seriously eroded.

HIV/AIDS – Generations and Gender

That campaign must reach girls as well as boys. At present, in sub-Saharan Africa, adolescent girls are six times more likely to be infected than boys. That is something which should make all of us African men deeply ashamed and angry.

Kofi Annan, 26 April 2001, Africa Leaders Summit on HIV/AIDS

There is plenty of literature and research on the impact of HIV/AIDS. There are terrifying statistics about the loss of human capital, especially in Africa. Zambia cannot train enough teachers to replace those who are dying each year from AIDS. Health, education, transport, core industries like mining and agri-business, together with key public services, face decimation in the Southern African region. The response to date has been to recruit key workers from other regions where possible and/or affordable. Botswana has recruited teachers and other professionals from Guyana (the poorest country in the Caribbean which can ill afford to lose professionals), yet they may have similar infection rates to those they have been hired to replace.

What exactly have male teachers who are infected with HIV/AIDS done? Many of them have infected the girls and young women they teach. Reports from South Africa early in 2001 reported that schools are unsafe for adolescent women. Demands for sexual favours from teachers and male students, together with the real danger of sexual assault and rape, make pursuing education a daunting prospect.

The situation in schools is part of a broader pattern. Typically it is older men who have knowingly or unknowingly infected young women. They have used their traditional cultural authority over women – especially young women – to demand sex. The 'sugar daddy' to a young woman needing funds to pay her school or university costs, the senior civil servant who demands sexual favours in return for promotion, the HIV-positive man who believes that sex with a virgin will cure him. This fabric of sexual inequality is coyly referred to as '"age mixing", typically between older men and young women or girls' (Global AIDS Epidemic Update – UNAIDS, December 2000).

Those responsible are the husbands, fathers, uncles, brothers, neighbours and community members that all of us know. Yet young women are blamed for their fate, labelled as precocious, promiscuous, having their values and morals eroded by globalisation and alien culture. Not identifying men's behaviour as the key is the real scandal. It means that a generation of girls and young women are paying with their lives.

In 1990 Amartya Sen identified the absence of one hundred million women from the global population. This is caused by a combination of factors: selective abortion of female foetuses, infanticide, neglect of the girl-child, complications in early pregnancy and child-bearing. Disproportionate infection with HIV/AIDS is another factor that must now be added to the list.

HIV/AIDS – the 'too hard box'

Children and young people are already bearing the brunt of the HIV/AIDS pandemic. Over 13 million children have been orphaned as a result of AIDS. Child and sibling headed households are an increasingly common feature in sub-Saharan Africa. The growing presence of street children is testimony to this. A young African woman (herself part of a sibling headed household) told me that in the capital city the government rounded up the street children to return them to their families – but of course there were no families for most of them to go back to.

What will happen when the impact of HIV/AIDS begins to be acknowledged and understood? Who will teach in schools, who will care for the sick, who will work in essential industry and commerce, who will farm the land, build the homes, care for children and be role models? Children and young people are already doing it for themselves but without the support and services they need.

Agricultural extension workers need to help the young subsistence and cash crop farmers. Professions like teaching, nursing, the law and medicine need to rethink how people get the necessary training and education. The transfer of skills and knowledge across the generations becomes an urgent imperative. High school graduates as teacher and nurse aides, articled clerks for the legal profession, apprenticeships, private sector and industry required to make young counterpart learning on the job compulsory?

Decision-makers and leaders are paralysed with fear and lack of comprehension. Life will never be the same again in those countries whose human and social capital continues to be decimated. Brave, bold, lateral thinking 'outside the box' is needed now at policy and programme levels to address the emergency. Children and young people must be fully participating actors in the partnerships that need be created, fast, to maintain development.

Solutions – the Way Ahead

Participation is a right

Parties shall assure to the child who is capable of forming his or her own views the right to express those views freely in all matters affecting the child, the views of the child being given due weight in accordance with the age and maturity of the child.
Convention on the Rights of the Child (CRC), Article 12:1

Young people are empowered when they make an informed decision freely, take action based on that decision and accept responsibility for the consequences of that action. Empowering young people means creating and supporting the enabling conditions under which young people can act on their own behalf, and on their own terms, rather than at the direction of others.

Commonwealth Plan of Action for Youth Empowerment, endorsed by Commonwealth Heads of Government, 1999.

The Benefits

Throughout the 1990s a common global agenda emerged through world summits and conventions. A focus on human development reflects recognition that economic growth alone does not improve quality of life or sustain democracy. Agreed common objectives of equality, development and citizenship were embodied in the UN Global Agenda of the UN Millennium Special Assembly, 2000.

The benefits of youth participation are multiple and not solely for young people themselves. Social inclusion, resulting in cohesive communities, solid support and engagement in national development, is clearly desirable. Institution-building and social cohesion are at least as important for nationally owned development processes as electoral democracy. World Bank research covering 192 countries found that 64 per cent of economic growth could be attributed to human and social capital (World Bank, 1996).

The target year for development objectives agreed at various international fora in the 1990s, and at the Millennium Summit, is 2015. 15–40 year olds are the most active age group of trainers, technicians and wealth creators at the local level. *It is today's 0–25 year olds who will be driving the process by 2015.* Their capacity to do so depends on practical decision-making experience.

- Up to two-thirds of the population of developing countries is under 30 years old. There is no alternative to targeting young people in development strategies. There are no alternatives to young people as the principal actors on the ground.

- AIDS deaths are one reason why skills-transfers from the older generation – both within families and in schools – are declining and are insufficient for the task ahead. Another is the importance of new technologies, including IT. Here the skills transfers are if anything being reversed: the younger generation is teaching the older.

- Fighting HIV means educating the under-30s, who account for over 60 per cent of those infected. Young people have a central role as peer educators and as evaluators of strategy. They know whether behavioural change has been achieved, and why.

Traditionally, the dichotomy has been between sectoral participation (education, workplace), and periodic, formal political participation (for example, voting). What is lacking is ongoing participation in decision-making.

One of the weakest links [between economic and social development] ... *is the lack of appropriate institutions for integrated policy frameworks. Such institutions 'should provide for the active participation of social actors ... to facilitate the 'visibility' of the social effects of economic policies.*

UN ECLAC, 2001

- *Participatory situation analysis* puts all stakeholders in command of more information – government, civil society organisations and young people.

- *Inclusive institutions* facilitate links between macro- and meso-economic policies; for example, employment strategies engage with the environment faced by firms. This attains a better social and economic return on both private investment and development assistance (such as micro-credit and enterprise skills training).

- *Multi-sectoral youth policies* 1) co-ordinate efforts across the state and civil society; 2) rationalise personal and institutional trade-offs between income generation and skills development for young people; 3) pool the statistical capacities of all government departments, so that realistic goals can be set and progress can be monitored.

Overcoming the Democratic Deficit – Together

Across the globe, younger generations are deprived of a sense of fully belonging to society. This does not reflect the potential of young people in development. Rather, it is a symptom of under-engagement itself. Only systematic participation can gain momentum, and revitalise a whole society. This is why one-off consultations and token youth representation is inadequate – nowhere more so than in youth policy itself. When involved in the design, implementation and evaluation of public policy, young people know their participation has been substantive. We must aim at nothing less.

In preparation for the UN Special Assembly on Children in September 2001, community, national, regional and international consultations are taking place. Some are aimed at the general child and youth population; others, like the African Movement of Working Children and Youth, seek to gather the views and inputs of children and young people living and working on the streets of 16 African countries. The impetus of the UN General Assembly Special Session has seen an explosion of interest in participation. Unfortunately it is not the norm in relation to those under 18 or those aged 18–30 in many countries.

However, the impact of young people's positive experience in the consultations is not transitory. Workshops, community forums, on-line forums, the 'Say Yes to Children' campaign and many different interventions will highlight and demystify the way in which policy is made and reveal to young participants how they can make their voices and opinions heard. The engagement of young people in formulating national youth policy in Commonwealth countries has done the same. These are foundation lessons in skills for a lifetime as an active citizen in a democracy.

The democratic deficit describes the gap in current development theory, the lack of participation by the poor in contributing to democratic policy dialogue on poverty and related issues. Participation skills are learned – they don't just happen. Development theorists and practitioners know that without participation and ownership by target groups the impact of interventions will be limited. Throughout the poverty reduction frameworks and strategies of donors runs the exhortation to involve the poor in designing solutions. Imagine if children and young people in poor and marginalised communities were part of youth and community action that practiced genuine participation. Would there be a democratic deficit? International development targets agreed by the UN and the international development community would have a head start. Between 2001 and 2015 (the time frame for achieving international development targets) they would engage increasingly mature young people and young adults who were able to take a full and active role in sustainable development regardless of their poverty. Young people's participation is win–win – there are no losers.

Chapter 2 of this book, contributed by Steve Mokwena, builds on a paper presented to Commonwealth Youth Ministers in 1998. The paper explored the theme 'Participation in decision-making: the empowerment of young people as the civil society of the twenty-first century'.

Mokwena brings to light the changing theory and practice of youth participation – the move from an approach in which young people's participation is defined within limits prescribed by adults towards a new paradigm of youth empowerment. He argues that it is necessary to build on post-liberation and independence democracy by engaging young people and that ensuring that young people are part of mainstream civil society is necessary to consolidate and deepen democracy.

He examines institutional, attitudinal and mythological barriers to participation. He points to the mythology of young people as apathetic and lacking motivation. The reality is that young people have their own civil society of sometimes formal and sometimes informal associations. However, this is either not recognised or not valued by adult society. Adults' perception is that young people are doing 'nothing' if they are not engaged in things defined as worthwhile by adults. Overcoming stereotyping (which of course is not a one way street) is a challenge for advocates to overcome.

Chapter 3, written by Indira Ravindran and Laila Duggan, presents a series of case studies from a wide range of organisations. Invitations were sent through the Partners for Youth Participation networks. Our intention was to feature examples from different regions of the world, to be gender-balanced and reflect a range of organisations from youth-initiated NGOs to international agencies.

The chapter examines a diverse range of organisations that provide positive models of young people's participation. They range from Bluepeace, a youth initiated and led environment NGO in the Maldives, to government-supported programmes in Papua New Guinea where the outreach of youth workers enabled the Husena village youth to make safe water accessible to their community. The spin-offs from this youth action transformed traditional relationships between the generations and created dialogue, awareness and action. The International Planned Parenthood Federation (IPPF) created a environment for genuine youth participation in its governance mechanisms with a Youth Advisory Council leading the process.

Successes in youth-based social movements are hard to find in well-documented form. The transitory nature of youth (albeit ranging from 15–30-years-old), and the practice and tradition of youth and development workers, means that 'doing' rather than recording, documenting and analysis is the norm. However, as can be seen in Chapter 3, there is diversity and richness of experiences and information. In analysing common themes from these successes key principles and lessons emerge: the importance of providing opportunity, not charity; the multiplier effect that even small initiatives can generate; and maintaining focus and passion as essential for sustaining participation.

Chapter 4, contributed by Charlotte Barran, features a collection of profiles of people from different generations. They share their personal experiences, and discuss pathways to participation and empowerment. PYP invited people to share their personal experiences of participation as a young person. The aim was to hear about who or what motivates individuals to participate, and the factors that make participation difficult or easy.

The chapter features nine personal profiles, together with an analysis, drawing conclusions, through personal testimony, of the enabling conditions that make participation possible and effective. A comparison of participation experience over 60 years examines the impact on people's subsequent life choices.

Charlotte Barran asserts there exists a 'set of circumstances which drives a person to become a young activist'. This is not dependent upon education or social status but is much more fundamental, 'a basic recognition of the need to participate in society and positive relationships with adults'. Thus the context and circumstances that individuals describe vary enormously but critical factors emerge that created a supportive and enabling environment for participation.

Finally, in Chapter 5 Kumi Naidoo presents a typology of young people's participation at macro-, meso- and micro-levels. It looks at both limited and substantial levels of participation and, importantly, how these fit into current concepts of active citizenship. The macro-level can be characterised as young people's concerns about why the world is the way it is; if change needs to happen, then how and where do they articulate their views and ensure that they are heard? The meso-level is about doing the right thing and the smart thing, especially in terms of policy and ensuring that desired outcomes are achieved with young people's engagement. This engagement must happen not simply by involving young people in consultations on policy but by ensuring that they have a real role in formulation, implementation and monitoring. Lastly, at the micro-level, young people want to do real things for real people. They need opportunities to put their energy, creativity and passion into action with tangible results.

In his analysis Naidoo examines the range of challenges and opportunities facing young people and civil society to create genuine participation for mutual benefit. He points out that even amongst the most marginalised and socially excluded young people there is still diversity and differentiation. Gender is a critical factor in this analysis as young women often become invisible and assumptions are made that either the 'women's' or 'youth' agenda will capture their needs. The reality is often that neither do so and they fall through the gap.

Youth leadership and partnership with other generational cohorts, especially those with a different experience of values formation, are important. Young people are growing up in a period of globalisation – one in which technology and geopolitics continue to change rapidly. They will influence new thinking, and become both the engine and the implementers of new paradigms of development and democracy. Lastly, Naidoo gives us 'GRACES' (gender equity, racial and religious tolerance, age and ability, class, community and caste, ethnicity and socially exclusion). He identifies these as key areas for social action that equip us all to overcome the challenge of intersectorality.

This book comes to you from a community of practitioners – itself described by Friedman in *The Lexus and the Olive Tree* as the most appropriate forum for creating new concepts for social policy in globalisation. We hope the experiences of young people, their advocates, mentors and partners will provide insights which can be acted upon. The transformation of generational relationships is a formidable challenge. It is an imperative but also an enormous opportunity for benefits that no-one can afford to ignore.

Chapter 2

Deepening Democracy: Meeting the Challenge of Youth Citizenship*

Steve Mokwena

Youth Participation: a Democratic Gift and an Imperative

Young people can build a democratic and prosperous world. They can overcome the barriers of the past, build on the strong tradition of co-operation and realise the value of self-reliance and enterprise. They should cultivate the courage to change the present and become partners in shaping a hopeful future.

Picture a society where all citizens, young and old, are informed about and engaged in all major issues that affect their lives. Adults and young people working together; debating, grappling with problems, crafting solutions and jointly deciding on how resources should be generated and allocated – a robust democracy where all people exercise their right to select, and hold accountable, those who speak and act on their behalf, and where all people have an equal opportunity to have a sustainable livelihood. Imagine adults and young people working together to build a thriving society from the ground up – contributing to peace and prosperity from the community level, to the national level, to the global level. This vision is inextricably tied to the values of democracy, liberty, justice and equity that are the fundamental values shared, at least in theory, by the community of nations and articulated in various United Nations Declarations.

These values underpin a collective determination to build strong thriving societies that can meet the challenges of a rapidly changing world. This is a challenge that can only be met when societies commit themselves to investing in the creation of a competent, creative, caring and contributing citizenry.

Yet today democracy is in grave danger. Many young people are disengaged from civic and political participation. They do not have the confidence in their capacity to be part of the political process in order to effect change.

The concept of youth participation is emerging as a central idea in the youth development discourse. It is a fresh way of engaging young people as central actors in the development equation – architects of their own personal development and in that of their communities and society in general.

Taking on this challenge, Commonwealth Youth Ministers meeting in Kuala

---

*This paper draws on a paper prepared for the Commonwealth Youth Ministers Meeting held in the Solomon Islands, September 2000.

Lumpur in 1998 made a clear and unprecedented commitment to provide resources and opportunities for young people to play an important role. By endorsing the Plan of Action for Youth Empowerment (PAYE), 54 Commonwealth governments committed themselves to the ideal of enfranchising young people – working with them and preparing them to assume responsibility for their lives and for the collective destiny of their communities and nations.

Developing this vision further, the World Meeting of Youth Ministers in Portugal largely endorsed these commitments in 2000. We can hope that this is more than a symbolic political gesture. It is a commitment to unleash the resources and creativity of young people – to place young people at the centre of creating solutions to the problems of poverty, social exclusion and the real threat of a disintegrating social fabric.

> *We believe in the liberty of individuals, in the equal rights for all citizens regardless of race, colour, creed or political belief and in the inalienable right to participate by means of free and democratic political processes in framing the society in which they live.*
>
> **Harare Declaration, 1991**

Barriers to Citizenship for Young People

However compelling, the idea of young people as full participating citizens is difficult to realise. This is in part because of the way societies have come to define the role of young people. In many communities young people are seen as deficient and problem-ridden – a group in society that should be controlled, fixed and for the most part seen and not heard. Many accept without question that young people are physically and mentally unsuited to handle the 'delicate' and 'complex' issues of power. Until recently, such ideas have been buttressed by academic theories that many have come to accept as the truth.

Young people as adults in waiting

Despite mounting evidence of young people's energy and contribution in many different aspects of society, 'youthfulness' and age are still used as a justification for excluding young people from decision-making. Major social institutions – the family, the school, community organisations, religious institutions and political parties – have yet to fully embrace the idea of young people as capable stake-holders and partners.

After carefully reviewing the theoretical underpinnings of most government policies on youth, Australian social scientists, Watts, Bessant and Sercombe,[1] conclude that societies and adults resist the participation of young people because it threatens their power. They argue that the abilities of young people are largely ignored as 'Theoreticians and practitioners [politicians] have yet to deal seriously with the adulthood of young people [the fact that young people are capable of responsibility], and the evidence that their exclusion from participation is a function of power, not innate developmental capacity'.

The widely held notion of youth as 'adults in waiting' serves to justify their relegation to a peripheral role in mainstream political processes. This analysis is affirmed eloquently by the sociologist Mike Males in his compelling book, *The Scapegoat Generation*.[2] Males argues that young people can be compared to other disenfranchised groups (women, ethnic minorities, and gay and lesbian people) who have been denied a place at the table throughout much of our recent political history. He asserts that in modern society: 'Young people are the last group we are allowed to systematically exclude.'

Gender inequality

Notwithstanding Males's observation about modern *ideals* on categorical exclusions, sexual discrimination is still rife all over the world. This is one of the most formidable barriers to youth participation. Its effects are indirect as well as immediate, impacting as it does on young women's education, self-confidence and reproductive health – to name but three determinants of social engagement.

The myth of youth apathy

One of the more frequently used justifications for excluding young people is the entrenched myth of youth apathy – young people are frequently portrayed as lacking motivation to become involved. This myth is captured most aptly in the media hype about 'Generation X' syndrome, which describes young people as a socially inert, self-absorbed group with little or no interest in the political process.

The young should sing, scream, paint their faces, go out into the streets, fill the squares, and demonstrate against lies, deceit, and shamelessness. The young should – while accepting the indispensable limits to freedom, the only way freedom can be real – fight against the abuse of power. ... Defence of freedom and alertness to its betrayal are democratic duties that we cannot neglect whether we are young or not. Moreover, protesting against the ethical slips of morally incompetent authorities is not only a way of studying and learning, but also a way of deepening knowledge and strengthening the roots of democracy. **Paulo Freire**

No-one bothers to ask if traditional political processes and institutions are open and accessible enough for young people (or anyone else for that matter) to want to be a part of them.

Young people as a problem

The most powerful barrier to young people's participation is the problem-based approach that has driven youth policy and programming since the 1960s. Young people were seen as a liability and threat that had to be contained with punitive and controlling social policies. Current efforts to work with young people are sometimes over-burdened as they fail to recognise the potential contributions of young people to social development. Many policy-makers and programmers think that we should first 'fix' young people, then develop them, and maybe then they can have the opportunity to participate.

> *Prevailing negative social attitudes of young people in many countries tend to give rise to ideologies that condemn and contain rather than encourage and empower young people. For many adults, allowing children [and young people] greater power is seen as a threat to the power relations between adults and young people.*   **Edna Smith**

Our challenge is to overturn these popular stereotypes about young people. To argue for a stronger link between young people's participation, their development and their capacity to influence positive change. Rather than just containing, c-ontrolling or ignoring them, societies have to invest in them – invest in the build-ing of a competent citizenry. Advocates of youth participation face the even bigger challenge of developing a sound knowledge and an evidence base that demon-strates young people's capacities for contribution, rather than making unsubstanti-ated claims or idealising young people without providing useful tools and strategies.

Investing in Young People: Building an Effective Citizenry

Over the years, we have seen the emergence of a more developmental and positive approach to working with young people. This approach is motivated by the under-standing that human and social capital is not built only when we solve problems – it is a product of careful investment.

As a leading proponent and pioneer of this approach, Karen Pittman,[3] asserts, problem-free is not fully prepared. By stopping young people from getting into trouble it does not follow that we are necessarily investing in their positive poten-tial. Nor does it follow that they are fully prepared to make a successful transition into adulthood, or to participate fully as citizens. Many societies have made remarkable advances in ensuring that children acquire a basic education and do not die of malnutrition or preventable diseases. However, many have yet to make comparable investments to ensure that young people have the capacities and opportunities to thrive and participate.

Linking Youth Development to Youth Participation

Even when young people are competent and prepared, they do not automatically participate in changing their communities or influencing the political life of their countries. In many Western countries that have comparatively sound educational and economic opportunities, young people still find themselves excluded and peripheral to the processes and activities that affect them and their communities.

In many developing countries (where young people are in the majority), policies assume that young people cannot participate until they have a good education, jobs, or are free of health problems. In other words young people have to be 'fixed', or social and economic situations have to be 'fixed', before young people can develop and participate.

This is not a viable approach. Young people cannot wait for fundamental changes in the social and economic environment before they take on the important role of contributing as citizens. Young people, especially those from troubled and under-served communities, do not have the luxury of standing on the sidelines; they must become fully engaged in the search for alternatives.

Thankfully we have seen a steady move away from a problem-based and punitive approach. More and more governments have acted to invest in the positive development of our young people. Governments are allocating increasing amounts of resources to provide young people with the skills and opportunities they need to help their nations confront poverty, lack of economic opportunity and HIV/AIDS. Many realise that participation is both a precursor to development and an outcome of development.

The Costs of Exclusion

Participation and exclusion are two sides of the same coin. When young people are not given the pathways and resources to participate in positive ways they can and often do create alternatives for themselves. UNESCO describes exclusion poignantly as a perverse state that forces young people into a state of marginality where they become mere bystanders to the world of work, education and decision-making. Forced into this state, many young people gravitate towards alternative and often negative sub-cultures where they have a sense of connection with their peers, and opportunities to gain income and social standing, albeit through very dangerous and dubious means.

The exclusion of young people also heightens social problems such as crime, violence, illiteracy and HIV/AIDS. It depletes the capacity of individuals and of societies to rejuvenate themselves.

But what is Participation?

Freedom is participation in power.   Cicero

Is youth participation a new term that describes old practices?

Put simply, youth participation is when young people are actively influencing processes, decisions and activities that affect their lives.[4] This is a broad definition and is often used interchangeably with the term empowerment. Many governments have now defined youth participation as a process or a state where young people can create choices, make informed decisions freely and take action based on that decision and accept responsibility for the consequences of their actions. More importantly 'empowerment is based on the belief that young people are the best architects for promoting their development, and in meeting the challenges and solving the problems faced in today's world and in the new millennium'.

At the heart of this concept is the critical idea that young people are not just victims, they are potential actors who can and *have* made significant contributions to society.

The implications for policy and programming are clear. The role of policy is to deepen the expectation that young people have a right to acquire the skills and resources they need to participate. Policy should also expand the political space for young people to acquire control and share in the exercise of power. Policy should also create a bridge between young people and adults in order to facilitate strong intergenerational relationships that ease the transfer of values and skills.

Working from this definition, it is clear that youth development and youth participation are inseparable.

One should emphasise that participation is a right and not an obligation. Young people should feel free to participate in activities that affirm them and should at no point be coerced to do so. It is also important to understand that all young people are not the same. Thus the capacity and inclination to participate varies from one young person to another. As Rajani points out, youth participation should be sensitive to the evolving capacities of young people. Such capacities are dependent on age and experience. We cannot expect a 10-year-old to do what a 19-year-old can do and vice versa.

Youth participation is not just about youth programmes

It is important to caution that although the language of youth participation and empowerment has been embraced widely, many think of it purely in terms of youth-based and youth-focused activities and not as broad concept that incorporates full enfranchisement into social, economic and political life. Thus many adult-led institutions are happy to have youth take a lead in very minimal ways. They do not, for example, appreciate that young people can be part of economic development.

> *Participation is an essential part of human growth, that is development of self confidence, pride, initiative, creativity, responsibility, co-operation ... this is whereby people learn to take charge of their lives and solve their own problems, is the essence of development.*   **Steve Burkey**

Balancing political participation and economic enfranchisement

It is also critical to have broader understanding of young people's participation and citizenship. Youth participation is not just about political participation. It is also fundamentally about economic citizenship. Therefore participation is also a process through which young people access the skills and opportunities to have an autonomous and sustainable livelihood. As we know, political participation without economic enfranchisement is a rather hollow ideal. We also have to be careful not to confuse participation with more 'acceptable' modes of civic engagement, traditionally restricted to heeding the law and showing allegiance.

It is also important to note that participation should always have the interests and the rights of young people at heart and not seek to abuse their goodwill. There is ample evidence that young people have been used as tokens and pawns in activities that harm their long-term development.

This not withstanding, there is growing evidence that young people's participation has very positive outcomes.

Identifying the Benefits of Youth Participation

There are three main benefits of youth participation. It is critical for the development of skills in young people; it is also critical for the programmes and services that are provided for them; and it is also critical for the development of the communities and societies where the young people live.

Benefits for youth: Through participation young people acquire essential skills.

Participation is integral to the development of confidence, character and competence. Participation builds connection to family, peers, significant adults and communities. Skills are at the core of what people need to live fulfilling lives and to navigate their way towards adulthood. Research, notably in the areas of education and reproductive health, has confirmed that young people – especially those in their early to and mid adolescence – learn best by doing. They learn by being engaged in making decisions about things that affect them in the context of organisations and activities that they care about.

> *Competence is learned through experience, not magically endowed as a certain time. Maturity and growth are an ongoing process, and are gained through participation. This is a virtuous cycle. The more one participates meaningfully, the more experienced, competent and confident one becomes, which in turn enables more effective participation.* **Rakesh Rajani**

Benefits for programmes and services: When young people are engaged in designing and implementing programmes they improve the capacity of such programmes to reach their goals. Young people provide useful information. They provide resources help the programmes implement relevant and creative strategies. They also make the programmes accessible and attractive to other young people.

For many years it was accepted that social institutions and programmes that are set up for young people, large and small.schools, hospitals, prisons and so on, should do things for young people and not with them. Unfortunately this is even true for many youth development programmes. Adults that are in charge of such programmes tend to treat young people as mere targets and beneficiaries. Thankfully, it is now accepted that young people's active participation is fundamental to the very success of strategies and programmes implemented for them. Much remains to be done to build a coherent body of knowledge that can advance our collective understanding of the centrality of youth participation to youth programmes.

Participation is also an outcome of the youth development process: When young people are fully engaged they tend to be more eager and willing to engage in other activities in their families, communities, and broader society. There is evidence that political skill of participation acquired during one's youth is part of a process of identity formation that shapes the individual's relationship to society in later life. Participation begets more participation.

Youth Can Take Action: Youth-Based Social Movements

The twentieth century saw the emergence of powerful social movements led by young people. Many of these were driven by the ideal of democracy and freedom for all. As we discuss the need to create spaces for young people to participate in society, we should be reminded that young people have often taken action to change conditions with limited support (and sometimes with no encouragement) from adults.

From the poverty-stricken streets of South Africa to the affluent ambience of Seattle, youth-based movements have demonstrated that young people are able and often ready to carve out political space independently. In this process, participation is not something given to young people – it is something they create.

> *With their energy, enthusiasm, strong wills and open minds, young people have been at the heart of many social movements in the past and the present.* **Premesh Chadran**

Over the years we have seen a proliferation of youth-initiated activities at a local and community level. These are not always large-scale and dramatic, yet they touch the lives of millions of young people everyday. Such participation happens within youth clubs, cultural groups, religious groups, and other institutions. Government polices and conventional youth development programmes sometimes ignore these efforts. For many young people they are the only thing that stands between them and the real abyss of alienation.

These activities often involve the development of critical youth leadership skills. They facilitate processes through which young people acquire the skills they need to be effective such as organising, advocacy, and resource mobilisation and fundraising. Youth leadership provides a core of skills that is essential to individual development while tapping into the resources of young people to take action.

At the heart of youth-based social movements is the concept of youth activism. Activism allows young people to take on the role of social actors – they identify issues that affect them and take purposeful action to change things. The late twentieth century saw the rise of powerful movements in areas such as the environment, anti-racism, economic and social justice, and gay rights. These remain important movements that will affect the nature of political discourse in many countries for many years to come.

Another key example of independent youth action is youth entrepreneurship. This typically denotes activities that are involved in supporting young people to set up their own businesses or to create jobs. It is important to mention that entrepreneurship is not limited to youth businesses; it is sometimes used to include innovative actions by young people in the area of social development.

Many researchers agree that the significance of youth engagement, be it large-scale or small scale, explicitly political or not, is that it offers opportunities, motivation and capacity-building.

Grassroots activity led and initiated by young people, or in partnership with caring adults, represents *opportunities* for engagement. Engagement is a stepping-stone into broader community life and a gateway to civic and associational life beyond schools and family.

Second, it provides *motivation* for youth to be engaged in something that benefits people other than themselves. Young people become aware about issues that affect them and their communities – they get to grasp the nature of the complexities and possible solutions.

Third, it provides young people with *skills and capacities* to do more. As a young person gains skills, experience and knowledge, they increase their ability to effect change.

Examples of good practice

While many governments and social institutions are struggling with the idea of youth participation and other perhaps even questioning its usefulness, there are some good examples of exemplary practice. Below are a few examples of good initiatives that promote youth participation.[5]

Youth parliamentarians in Uganda

Under the provisions of the National Youth Statute of 1993, and the parliamentary act of 1995, five young people between the ages of 18–30 are elected to the national government in Uganda. The law also states that one of the five young people should be a female representative, representing the interests of young women. This provides a powerful platform for young people to raise their concerns and influence policy at all levels. The young people elected, who come from different regions in the country, have been effective in representing their peers. They organise special sessions where they lobby other parliamentarians. They have also made significant strides in organising young people in different communities and taking their recommendations to decision-makers. Youth representatives have a much deeper connection with their constituencies than most of the adult parliamentarians.

Co-management in Lithuanian Youth Policy

Lithuania as an emerging democracy after the fall of the Soviet Union has been working on developing policies and systems that facilitate the effective participation of young people in social development. Critical in this process has been the principle of co-management – young people working with government officials to design and implement policies and programmes. This process is facilitated mainly through the State Council of Youth Affairs (State Council). Through the State Council young people from youth NGOs elect six members who then sit alongside six representatives from different government ministries (these are usually deputy ministers from key ministries). The chairperson of the State Council is a government representative and the deputy chairperson is a representative of the youth NGO sector. Decisions within the State Council are made through a simple majority vote, thereby giving young people equal power to their adult counterparts. The State Council also employs a secretariat staff responsible for implementing its decisions. In 2001, the State Council was responsible for programmes aimed at strengthening youth NGOs, integrating young people into the economy, preventing drug abuse, suicide and crime, and providing leisure opportunities for rural youth. Within this system of co-management, young people are fully involved in making decisions about the design, funding, implementation and evaluation of programmes.

Brazil: Engaging underprivileged young people[6]

In 2000, Brazil celebrated the 10th anniversary of its Statute on the Child and Adolescent. Participants emphasised the importance of youth participation in NGO and government activities and focused, specifically, on encouraging young people's involvement in the Municipal Child and Adolescent Rights Council. Five young persons, aged 15 to 20 years, are now formal members of the sixteen-member Rights Council. These young people are involved in programme planning, implementation and evaluation; they are given a voice in designing public policies that are geared to adolescents and children.

In order to bolster support for youth participation, programme leaders have been working with the media to strengthen the concept of youth empowerment. They have also been promoting the concept among government leaders.

Projects designed to foster wider youth involvement encounter serious constraints. Given the economic conditions in Salvador, many children are forced to focus on earning money for their families. Faced with these demands, they do not set a high priority on participation in discussion groups. In addition many, particularly among the poorer groups, are frustrated with government performance and do not anticipate tangible benefits from participation. Meanwhile middle class youth are largely uninterested. Generally, they consider government policies for youth as destined solely for the poor.

In response, some of the social projects provide young people with scholarships so that they do not have to focus on earning an income. Others provide employment for young people when they are older than 16 years. Additionally, there are continued attempts at stimulating group activities, emphasising situation analysis and encouraging young people to formulate solutions.

The Commonwealth Youth Programme's support for national youth policies

The Commonwealth Youth Programme (CYP) has been critical in supporting Commonwealth member governments to develop a dynamic and compelling vision for young people in decision-making.

Through the Youth Policy 2000 programmes, the CYP has assisted over 40 member governments in developing legislative instruments and policy documents that place young people at the centre of their government's agendas. In addition many have worked to develop national plans of action to implement these policies. The youth policy process is unique in that it provides resources and space for young people to articulate themselves and to work together across ethnic, racial, socio-economic and political lines. This has been a useful process of training and emulating the democratic process itself.

Challenges

Although experiments in youth policy development have been positive in the main, there are some challenges. Here are some challenges to watch out for:

- **The dangers of window dressing**

First, while member governments have accepted the broad principle of youth participation, many do not fully embrace the idea of young people as actors in their own right. Young people are often put forward as window dressing with little decision-making capacity.

- **Arbitrary selection**

Second, some governments do not apply democratic principles in the selection and deployment of young people. Many representatives are not elected; they are hand-picked without any consideration of their ability to represent their peers. Individuals are selected and put forward even when they do not have any substantial connection to youth organisations or track record. Thus they are unable to promote the interests of their peers adequately.

- **Co-option**

Third, once selected, young representatives can become the official spokespersons of the ministry or the department responsible for youth affairs. As they depend on the government for their resources and continuing participation, they often shy away from taking positions that are controversial or contrary to those held by the government – even when these go against the interests of young people. Co-option does not in fact serve governments, as it deprives them of much needed alternative perspectives and insights that can only come from an independent youth voice.

- **Weak structures – crisis of legitimate representation**

Fourth, many of the youth representatives come through the ranks of National Youth Councils, National Youth Forums, National Youth Commissions, etc. These structures claim the legitimacy to put forward representatives on the grounds that they are linked to grass-roots organisations of young people. It is assumed that they have a mandate to consult and engage youth constituencies as and when necessary. However, in some cases, these structures do not have the capacity or inclination for work with young people on the ground. After a while it is unclear who they represent – all young people, organised youth only, or simply themselves.

- **Gender Inequality**

Fifth, without careful planning, youth structures are liable to display the same gender inequalities as other institutions. Young women within them may play a token role, rather than being active and equal members. The causes can lie in adult organisational culture or in young society itself. The consequences are impaired legitimacy and greatly reduced capacity to confront society's most pressing concerns.

- **Gate-keeping and centralisation**

Sixth, structures created to facilitate youth representation in the political process may find themselves in the position where they compete for resources and space with other civil society organisations. Instead of becoming vehicles that galvanise young people into action by injecting resources and by using their governments in strategic ways, they become gatekeepers by centralising the flow of resources and opportunities. This often leads to undemocratic tendencies that make them vulnerable to nepotism and bureaucratisation.

Opportunities: Consolidating the Gains

Fortunately, there is an opportunity to learn from these challenges and build on the strong commitment of youth leaders, governments and civil society organisations. There is a wealth of experience and goodwill that can be built on to improve practice.

Developing clear democratic criteria and procedures for the selection and deployment of youth delegates: It is important for governments to develop and agree on a broad framework for the democratic selection of youth delegates and representatives to international conferences. Chief among selection criteria should be a) the ability of representatives to articulate the aspirations of their peers, and b) their accountability to both their peers and others. Obviously such a framework should be sensitive to local conditions, but it must emphasise accountability and genuine representation. It should also allow for the regular replacement of delegates/ representatives.

Building a strong civil society that supports and promotes youth participation:
Creating structures for co-ordination and lobbying on behalf of youth is an important part of promoting youth participation. But these are only useful if they can do very specific things. The first is to mobilise grassroots support in a way that advances the ability of youth to be involved in their development and that of their communities. They must also bolster the efforts of NGOs and community based organisations (CBOs) by maximising their resources and political prominence. Thirdly and most importantly, they must advance the youth development agenda inside the government without becoming clients of the state and thus limiting the capacity of the political youth movement to lobby effectively for lasting social transformation.

Creating mechanisms for monitoring and evaluation of youth policies: Work is underway to create monitoring and documentation mechanisms that will enable governments see the progress that is being made. Attempts at evaluating progress will require the setting up of systems for data gathering and analysis. A direct role for young people in the design and operation of such assessment and evaluation exercises will be essential. This will bring a sense of ownership, commitment and genuine partnership between young people and their national governments.

Investing in the training and capacity building of youth leaders: Resources should be made available to ensure that young people brought into the system have adequate training and support to be able to meet challenges. Such training should emphasise democratic values and practice. It should also familiarise young people not just with the workings, traditions and objectives of their own countries, but also about how things work internationally.

Supporting research that demonstrates the capacity of young people to effect positive change: As noted, much of the resistance to youth participation comes from a misunderstanding of what young people can do, and actually do. Available data and research is understandably focused on problems. This ignores the positive reality of what young people are actually doing on a day-to-day basis. Without neglecting the problems, governments are encouraged to work with civil society bodies to generate research and knowledge on the nature and benefits of youth participation.

Creating strong adult–youth partnerships: Genuine youth participation is not possible or feasible without partnerships with adults. Research has proved over and over again that young people need to work together with adults in a respectful and mutually beneficial way. While young people need to have the space and the autonomy to take independent action they also need the guidance and support of caring and competent adults. Adults provide the invisible infrastructure behind youth action and engagement.[7] The capacity to provide apprenticeships for young people in areas such as political participation and governance is critical for the survival of democracy.

Promoting diversity and range: It is also important to support programmes that cover a range of activities and areas. Participation in faith-based organisations, in sports, and in culture is as important as participation in explicitly political activities. Fortunately, many governments are already making sizable investments in these areas. But others sometimes think of such activities as insignificant and not linked to the serious business of building democracy.

Promoting youth participation as a public idea: Finally, it is important to promote the idea of young people's participation and citizenship as a public idea. This is a principle that can be embraced by all people, not just by the select few who work with young people. The simple fact that young people can and should be architects of change must be ingrained in all areas of public life. It must be reflected most explicitly in education policy, as well as in all other areas of social planning and development that affect young people.

Conclusion – Youth Participation and Social Change

Our capacity to promote youth participation is dependent in part on our understanding of the symbiosis between youth development and the development of society in general. Youth development is inextricably tied to young people's capacity and willingness to participate at a micro-level (in programmes) and at a macro-level. The level and nature of young people's participation is in itself a marker for a society's development.

Therefore, the capacity of a society or a community to maximise young people's participation as citizens in social, political and economic life indicates the extent to which that society can flourish. Young people are barometers through which we can measure the level of social cohesion, democratisation or the lack thereof and thus the potential for positive change.

Youth participation presents a radically different and progressive perspective on the role of young people in society. Through participation, young people cease to be passive recipients of services or passive victims of indomitable social and political forces. Within this progressive perspective, young people are seen as stakeholders with distinct and legitimate interests and thus are entitled to share in the exercise of power at all levels.

The bold investments made in pursuit of young people's participation are already yielding visible benefits. Our challenge is to sharpen our tools and consolidate our infrastructure to make sure that young people's participation stays on the agenda of governments, businesses and adult-led civil society organisations.

Youth participation is our greatest hope for lasting social transformation. It lies at the core of our mission to create compassionate, sustainable and equitable societies where all people can thrive.

Notes

1. Watts, Bessant and Sercombe (1998). *Youth Studies – A Perspective*. Melbourne: Longman.

2. Mike Males (1996). *The Scapegoat Generation*.

3. Karen Pittman and Merita Irby (1996). International Youth Foundation.

4. Rakesh Rajani (1999). *An approach to adolescent participation*. UNICEF.

5. Examples from Uganda by D. Obbo and Lithuania by A. Augastaitis are taken from a report on youth participation in decision-making commissioned by the Carnegie Young People Initiative in the UK and edited by Steve Mokwena.

6. The example from Brazil was taken from 'Adolescent Participation in Situation Assessment and Analysis', a paper by Joy Moncrieffe commissioned by UNICEF and CYP, 2001.

7. Steve Mokwena (2000). *Youth and Social Justice, New Designs*.

Chapter 3

Institutional Pathways to Empowerment

Indira Ravindran and Laila Duggan

Mahatma Gandhi, while still a young leader, said 'never underestimate the power of the individual to change the world'. While his own life was proof of this conviction, Gandhi, along with the other leaders of the Indian independence movement, dedicated most of his efforts to institutional and structural reform. Women and men who have 'changed the world' have done so through transforming institutions. Appropriately enough, the longest chapter in this book is dedicated to a survey of organisations whose mission and activities are aimed at youth empowerment, and the reform of debilitating political and civil institutions.

Ten organisations are featured in this chapter, and they each present a 'case study' of a particular project that has demonstrably led to skill-building and confidence-building in the young people involved. Between them, these ten case studies cover two international networks, four continents, seven countries, dozens of transformed communities and many more young lives. They stretch across a spectrum of issue areas, including: reproductive health; the global population problem; mainstreaming sustainable development in national life; HIV/AIDS; self-expression through art and photography; rural reconstruction; and young people creating new institutions on the strength of already successful youth programmes.

Steve Mokwena's discussion in Chapter 2 examines some of the social mechanisms that systematically exclude young people from the decision-making spheres of public life. Too often, they are constructed as 'objects' to be acted upon or passive targets for policies and decisions made elsewhere. When we see young people as scientists, parliamentarians, entrepreneurs, artists or writers, we treat them as exceptions.

We also tend to exceptionalise young people who are engaged in other, more distressing, 'adult roles'. We are daily inundated with soundbites and images of young people (sometimes barely out of childhood) as child soldiers, sex workers, child labourers, rag-pickers, gun-wielding murderers in suburban schools, juvenile delinquents and accidental parents. Yet we do not always question the structural disempowerment that assigns young people to these roles. We need enabling and supportive institutions that value each young life and its place in the community.

There is a vacuum in information on positive youth schemes and initiatives that aim to change the world or one community at a time. In presenting these case studies, we hope to begin to fill this vacuum. The experiences of these ten organisations and their affiliates bring hope and optimism to our collective aspirations. In keeping with the spirit of participation and openness underlying this publication, we have opted to let the stories speak for themselves, and have tried to limit our editorial intervention to a minimum. Each of the case studies stands alone, and stands well. Yet, taken together, they present an exciting canvas of common colours, textures, patterns and trends. We give a brief survey of the main themes at the end of this chapter.

Case Study 1

Drik: Out of Focus

Ten years ago, a small group of people in Bangladesh decided they would right a wrong. The Western media had created an image that was distorted and far from the truth. Their country was known for all the wrong reasons. It was to challenge that image that Drik was created.

The Sanskrit word stands for vision, inner vision, philosophy of vision. Drik was set up to provide a platform for photographers and writers of the majority world to present their vision. Adhering to its core concept, the organisation has grown from being a provider of images and text to being a media resource centre that challenges western hegemony. Drik stands tall amongst the image banks in the developing world. The in-house gallery holds several major international exhibitions every year. The Centre boasts a modern studio, photographic laboratories and a multimedia unit. It also operates as an Internet service provider.

Drik's social commitment is central to its work ethos. In fact, Drik's founder, Shahidul Alam, was a commercial and advertising photographer when he started documenting the popular resistance against Bangladesh's autocratic president, General Ershad, in 1987. This won him the Mother Jones Award in 1992. Alam founded Drik Picture Library (www.drik.net) in 1989; the Bangladesh Photographic Institute in 1990; Pathshala, the South Asian Institute of Photography (www.drik.net/pathshala), in 1998; Meghbarta (www.meghbarta.net), Bangladesh's first web-based news magazine, in 1999; Chobi Mela (www.chobimela. org), the first festival of photography in Asia in 2000; and Bangladesh Human Rights Network (www.banglarights.net) in 2001.

In keeping with its founding vision, Drik's training programmes range from providing education for working class children to training the region's brightest young photojournalists to operate at an international level through Pathshala. Through the first Bangladeshi web portal (http://bd.orientation.com), which Drik maintains, the original platform is now taking global shape.

Origins of 'Out of Focus'

On 4 October 1994, the Drik Picture Library Ltd. launched **Out of Focus**, a participatory photography initiative with young working class children. The goal was to assist the children in learning photography as a means for them to communicate their experiences and as a means for future employment.

Drik Picture Library works with several groups of children. The core group has 11 children, six girls and five boys. The children have since grown into young adults, one girl is 14 and the rest are 16- and17-years-old. The inspiration for **Out of Focus** is articulated in a statement by one of the children about the owner of a garment factory where many children died as a result of a fire. 'If I had a camera, I'd take his picture and put that guy in jail.'

We chose to work with the children from working families because we saw that there is no working class representation in mainstream media, and reporting on issues important for poor people is done from an urban middle class perspective. **Out of Focus** was an attempt to redress that bias.

Photography was chosen as a means for participation because, in a community where levels of textual literacy is low, images are the most powerful means of communication. Using photography was a way in which the children could readily articulate complex issues regarding their environment and social conditions in a direct manner.

Drik believes there are unique benefits of using photography as a means of participation and empowerment, particularly with young people. Even at a very early stage the children have made some very powerful statements using photography. They are becoming increasingly more articulate with words, and now combine words with images to get their ideas across.

Photography was also a means by which they could share their statements with their community. As a result, the children's exhibitions have belonged to the community and have had a lot of community participation.

Since its inception in 1994, **Out of Focus** has grown in strength as the children have developed their skills. Drik has become integrated with the immediate community because of our frequent and varied interactions with the core group of children. We have also tried working with other children, particularly in rural areas, but have observed that our proximity and frequent contact with the core group has meant that they have matured far more quickly than the rural group. The same applies to the other groups of urban children where we have not been able to integrate as well.

Achievements

The young participants of **Out of Focus** have become very responsible young men and women, and while they appreciate the opportunity they have received, they do not want to feel dependent on Drik and are trying to find ways of attaining self-sufficiency. They are, however, deeply attached to the organisation and are constantly looking for ways that would allow the organisation to prosper. We have an extremely warm relationship with the parents, and the children (no longer children really) look upon Drik as part of their extended family.

Since 1994, the children have had publications and exhibitions internationally. Several of them now work in a national television channel, two work at Drik and another works in a leading audio-visual NGO. The children have, therefore, established themselves at a professional level. Two of the children are now at college. The most significant development has been in the children's self-confidence and their heightened social awareness. Some of the children have taught their parents to read and write.

The children's photography and writing have been published in several international books and magazines. They have had two exhibitions at the United Nations building in New York, and one at the Photographers Gallery in London, besides three major exhibitions in Bangladesh. A new exhibition is scheduled in Dhaka for 23 March 2001. The children have been featured in television programmes in several countries. Audio-visual presentations by the children are being used in schools in Sweden for educational purposes. The work is also featured on the web: http://zonezero.com/magazine/essays/shahidulchildren/p0en.html and http://www.drik.net/chobimela2k/htmls/bangladesh/bdourlang/bdourlang.html.

People and organisations have been overwhelmed by the quality and the strength of the photographic work of the children participating in **Out of Focus**. The rural programme was initiated in collaboration with Save the Children USA, as it wanted to replicate the project. UNICEF bought 500 copies of the first publication for distribution. The audio-visual production was commissioned by Radda Barnen for educating school children in Sweden.

As I hold the calendar in my hands (I only got it an hour or so ago and have done nothing but look at it and share it with my daughter, since) I honestly can't tell you, for I cannot find the right words, what I feel about this initiative ... and the whole concept behind it. I cried tears of joy and sadness as I looked at what the pictures and the text said. God bless you and all those who are part of this ... give the young photographers a great big hug from me. In fact, I'll do it myself, for they have made me 'finalize' the thought that I need to visit Bangladesh again.
Zaheer Alam Kidwai, Media activist, Pakistan.

Resources

Out of Focus has been an ongoing independent initiative of Drik for nearly seven years. The first six weeks of the project was partially supported by the Arkleton Trust in the UK and UNICEF. Since then, Drik has allocated a significant part of its annual budget for the children's development, which includes their education, health care and social awareness. Besides receiving help in school subjects, they also work with sociologists and anthropologists on a regular basis. Some of this is provided on a voluntary basis by friends of Drik. Small donations have also been made by individuals. The children now generate some income from sales of their images. They are selling a 2001 calendar, which features their work, to raise monies for their upcoming exhibition.

Challenges

At Drik we feel strongly that one hindrance to any such participatory initiative stems from thinking of them as 'projects'. Projects have finite starting and end points. They require quantifiable outputs, which need to be justifiable on the basis of measurable inputs. These are children who are very much part of Drik's family. The usual question is, 'how is all this funded', yet the same question is never asked regarding our own children. The problem lies in treating them as 'special children' who are being salvaged. How does one measure a child's confidence? How does one quantify their ability to create spaces for themselves in a hostile environment where people are assessed on the basis of their family standing, the clothes they wear and the accents they have? How does one value the deep social commitment and the extremely high quality of journalism that the children obviously have? Iqbal has taught his mother to read and write. How much is that worth in money terms?

If in place of salvation, we looked upon it as addressing a situation of exploitation, where we ourselves are in normally in the exploitative role, perhaps we would look at the whole thing differently.

In monetary terms, of course, it has been difficult for a small organisation like Drik to sustain such a programme. Other unforeseen pressures came in the form of family illnesses, where Drik had to bear the bulk of the medical costs. One of the girls, Shapna, was married off by her father and later became pregnant, and we had to deal with the complications of a young pregnancy. Now that the children are going to college, their educational expenses are mounting. Since they find themselves in professional roles, it is important for them to be dressed smartly, so there are additional costs. However, the most significant area of conflict arises when they face class prejudice in work situations. Sometimes this prejudice is even found within Drik, where not everyone shares the Drik philosophy in the same way.

In the early stages, the children faced a lot of criticism from the community, who claimed that Drik was there merely to get some benefit of our own and the friendship wouldn't last. Over time, Drik and the children established their credibility within the community, on the strength of their commitment and the ongoing success of **Out of Focus**.

Case Study 2

collective echoes

Shabna Ali and M. Simon Levin

collective echoes (The Society for Collectively Echoing Culture in Public Space) is a small, non-profit organisation based in Vancouver, Canada. Emerging from a project initiative of Vancouver Multicultural Society, *collective echoes* outgrew its host organisation and became self-standing in 1999. An arts organisation that valued the voices of community and youth equally in the creation of public art, *collective echoes* initially aimed to provide young people with the opportunity to create public art, gain skills and experience and, more importantly, to find self-expression. The mission expanded to empower youth to educate the public about the role youth plays in healthy communities and to create learning opportunities for people to become cultural innovators.

Youth involvement

collective echoes, although originally conceived by adults, moved very quickly up the rungs of Roger Hart's ladder of youth participation (see Roger Hart, *Children's Participation: From Tokenism to Citizenship*, UNICEF). We asked ourselves hard questions: what decisions are these young people truly making? Are they decisions that will shape the organisation, or are they decisions that are relatively super-fluous? Ultimately, are the adults willing to give up power?

As an organisation that was serious about youth expression, we decided that young people needed to have an understanding of decision-making processes and be informed about the issues. All decisions had to be shared and no-one could act unilaterally without the consent of the group. To achieve this a consensus-building process was established in which all issues, big or small, were discussed until the group felt that they had enough information to support a decision. Individuals began with a personal 'check-in' that established sensitivity to each other's needs and concerns. All participants were expected to be accountable for their involvement and question themselves on whether their language and approach were inclusive and respectful of cultural difference.

If a particular issue did not greatly concern a member, they could remove themselves from the discussion and this made the consensual system feasible. But no-one was ever asked to support anything that they were fundamentally opposed to.

The co-mentorship model

Co-mentorship is based on the idea that every person can and should learn from interacting with the others. In order to allow the co-mentorship model to flourish, each person had to work from a place of strength and understanding; they had to have a specific area of knowledge (or niche) that was necessary to the creation of community-based public art. To accomplish this, we divided the public art projects into teams, each comprising an established artist, an emerging artist, a community developer, and an organisational leader. Each member therefore either had knowledge based on previous work, understanding of various perspectives (young emerging artists), knowledge of the community or organisational insights. This did not mean that each person was confined to these tasks, just that they were able to mentor their team members on that area.

public:untitled

public:untitled began by examining and questioning traditional ways of operating. In hiring the 13 young people who took part, we decided to:

- Post the position in the ordinary manner but also in places frequently accessed by socially excluded people;

- Allow people to apply without a formal resumé. This helped those young people who did not have access to computers or training on application skills;

- Conduct simple phone interviews that asked about the candidate's passion and vision for themselves. This served to narrow the applicants from 300 to 30;

- Invite the entire group of 30 in for a group interview in which games and art were the focus. We were looking for creativity, ability to work with different people, openness, willingness and compassion;

- A group of 20 were invited in for individual interviews. In an attempt to balance the power dynamic, they were asked to be prepared to interview the hiring team (a group of 5:3 adults, 2 youth).

The level of trust created from that process, both among the hiring team, and between the hiring team and the candidates, was immense. Many young people who did not get selected were so impressed that they continued to participate as volunteers or by joining the advisory group.

We recognised that cultural differences among the young people could pose a barrier to communication; with this in mind we sought diversity training. The diversity trainer we brought in from another multi-cultural organisation was also a young person. This immediately changed the power dynamic in the group and most of the participants were more comfortable and less intimidated, given her age.

If we were going to change power dynamics, then the administrative components traditionally held by adults had to include youth. We decided that the financial end of the organisation had to involve young people. One of the young people initially hired had an aptitude for numbers and developed an interest in the budgeting and finances. The same young person is currently still financial co-ordinator and she is training two new young people to take over the accounts. An adult volunteer accountant is still available, when necessary, to handle any questions or difficulties that arise. Obviously handing the financial accounts of an organisation with an operating budget of $750,000 to a young person with no formal training required much trust, openness and understanding from all parties involved.

Another task traditionally handled by adults is fundraising. Initially, in securing start up funds for *collective echoes*, adults generated all grants. Young people soon called into question how decisions were made on which companies would be supporting us financially. A sub-committee of the advisory group met to examine ethical funding principles; this group consisted largely of young people. This led to the creation of a set of ethical screens that *collective echoes* adopted in its funding operations. A fundraising team was developed, and was mentored on all elements of grant writing, corporate solicitations and cold calls. The small team quickly grew and young people originally mentored by an adult went on to mentor other young people.

Achievements

Below is a brief description of the organisation's temporary and permanent public arts projects:

THE MOUNT PLEASANT GOLF AND COUNTRY CLUB takes the form of an 18-hole miniature golf course linked through three sites in central Vancouver. By employing the metaphor of game, this public artwork invites the local community to play in a popular family-oriented activity while subverting the élitism associated with golf and country clubs. Each hole is artist-designed and evokes issues such as neighbourliness, crime, class disparity, youth culture and public transit.

ADVERTISING BODIES ALLIANCE (A.B.A.) addresses the use of our bodies as billboards in public space. A.B.A. believes that we have a right to be paid as human advertisements, when wearing clothing with corporate logos. Public performance interventions throughout Greater Vancouver involved handing out invoices to the public who were then encouraged to bill multinationals for their service.

FOUND YOUTH FOUND VOICES challenges the way youth culture is made into a commodity. It does this through sticker and poster campaigns and a series of public performances. The 'Wanted Youth' poster campaign targeted apathetic youth, challenging them to make a difference while offering ways to get involved.

WATERMARK consists of symbols designed and created by community members stencilled onto streets and sidewalks with road paint, following the path of lost streams in the Trout Lake neighbourhood. These personal voices speak out in resistance to the dominance of official and consumer signage in our visual environment.

SYSTEMS OF SUSTENANCE addresses issues of sustainability by focusing on the Coast Salish fish bone ceremony. This ritual returned salmon bones to the water to thank the salmon spirit and to ensure future bountiful harvests. A public performance involved three spirits with offerings of fish bones made of sodium bicarbonate, which bubbled and dissolved when dropped into False Creek. On another occasion, metal salmon shapes were installed on near 'Science World'. In progress is a monumental sculpture carved from three cedar stumps that will function both as rain catchers and nurse logs. Also an aboriginal medicinal garden is to be planted in nearby Creekside Park.

Another outcome of *public:untitled* was the emergence of the Teaching Team, made up of young art educators. The Teaching Team uses the educational principles of *collective echoes* among high school students. It develops curricula that aim to create entry points for groups of young people who might otherwise be overlooked. The team also introduces high school students to the role that contemporary art can play in social change. The Teaching Team has fulfilled ongoing contracts for the Contemporary Art Gallery and the Vancouver Art Gallery, and is consistently booked for youth conferences.

Although these achievements fulfill the initial mandate, other less tangible outcomes continue to have an impact. For instance, the dialogue that emerged from diversity training, and increased awareness about power and privilege has and will continue to impact on Vancouver.

Challenges

The greatest challenge that *collective echoes* faced was one of funding. In attempting to create a new model of working, *collective echoes* was charting new ground in Vancouver. This damaged our perceived credibility and made securing funds extremely difficult. Without the partnership of A.I.A. Arts in Action, and the initial organisational support of Vancouver Multicultural Society and the Vancouver Foundation, *collective echoes* would still be simply a dream. These organisations had the vision, the leadership and openness to assist us in creating *collective echoes*.

We were heavily reliant on a government grant that would pay the wages of most of the young people. This grant fell through after the interviews had taken place. Losing this grant meant that we had to restructure our budgets, teams, wages and work hours considerably. We were forced to compromise one of our fundamental principles: paying artists fair and reasonable wages. This shift affected the morale of the staff and the amount of time people could dedicate to the project, as most had to supplement their income with other paid work.

A few people, both young and old, left the project early. New people were brought into the process at varying stages, resulting in different levels of knowledge, understanding and communication skills. The co-mentorship model made it possible for these people to be brought on board quickly, as everyone was able to educate. However, those associated with the project the longest benefited most.

Another struggle for *collective echoes* throughout was establishing effective community connections. Many long-standing residents and community stakeholders were uncomfortable with youth-led sessions. Although the meetings were run fairly traditionally and facilitation skills were exemplary, our work was not seen as legitimate. It was not until the teams redesigned their approach, developing more playful methods and working from their own strengths that they made the necessary inroads. Scavenger hunts, contests, T-shirt making and cartooning workshops successfully bypassed the reluctant community members and attracted a younger audience that endeared *collective echoes* to community programmers. Ultimately the most successful community development was done within *collective echoes*.

Lessons learned

By living and working for our ideals to the fullest, we inevitably created a vulnerable organisation, one that required people to be sustained by their enthusiasm. Large doses of reality need to be part of the equation if this kind of model is to be replicated. Ideally, we would not have forged ahead without secured wage funding, or we would have greatly reduced the kind of public art pieces we were undertaking. But our desire to fulfill the original vision kept us focused on our early goals.

Dana Thorne – First Nations Woman, Youth Project manager for *public: untitled*

I am honoured to be able to share my thoughts and feelings about this project with others. I ask that you take the time to really read what I am saying, and not to just skim it over and nod, acting as if you understand everything that I have written. With that in mind, let me start by telling you a little about my background and myself.

My name is Dana Thorne and I am a twenty-year-old First Nation's woman who was born, raised and spent most of my life on Vancouver Island. I am a member of the Cowichan Tribe, which is the biggest tribe in British Columbia. Growing up with the identity of a Native Indian was hard for me. I caught myself always claiming the identity of my Italian grandfather, and feeling guilty in doing so. I would always add at the end of my sentences, in a quiet voice which faded out each and every time, the words, 'and. ... Part ... native'. I always felt blessed that my family was all fair-skinned compared to many other First Nation's people, and that my skin colour was even more fair than the colour of my family's skin.

Society has attempted to understand what it is like to be a minority. We now have Aboriginal Day, and Multicultural Week, and people protesting and fighting to no longer have racism among us. I give thanks and acknowledge those who try to under-

stand, and think they understand, but racism goes much deeper then a remark on the street or a refusal to serve those of colour. There is the racism of the subconscious mind, a racism that I have just become aware of, or should I say that I have finally accepted, because of the mentoring and the open discussions that take place here at collective echoes. *I can try to explain, but only people who are open and aware can understand. I am talking about how when we, as minorities, are in meetings or talking, people don't always listen. However, if a person of the dominant culture presents the same idea, it is often heard louder, even though we had just spoken the same language not even five minutes earlier. This is what society and people don't always understand or want to admit. I too am guilty of having prejudice, and I too did not want to admit, but when working with a project that truly deals and addresses diversity as* public: untitled *does, it becomes a part of reality that you can no longer ignore in society. I now understand and must change this prejudice against my own people that I hold within.*

My understanding of how society tries to accept minorities comes from the experiences that I had working in my first job. At the age of sixteen I was confronted with a job posting for a bank; they were looking to hire aboriginal people. I applied and got the job a week after my interview. I thought it was amazing to have my first job be in a bank instead of a fast food restaurant. The job was very professional and precise on how things had to be done. I would at times forget to do things here and there, but that was only because I was still learning. My supervisor soon told me that I was hired only because I was native and now I had to prove myself. I felt worthless and called the area manager to complain. He assured me that she didn't mean it that way and it must have just come out wrong, but he would have a talk with her. I was then transferred to another branch, and in my evaluation the woman wrote that I had a tendency to do things my own way and not the way the bank liked it. I told her that it was only because I would forget to do things sometimes, like fill out a deposit slip when someone hadn't done so, but she wouldn't hear it. I felt like I didn't have a voice and that I didn't matter. I felt that I was just there as an accessory. I was there to make the bank look better, because they now had First Nation's people working for them. I continued to work for the bank and just accepted that I didn't have a voice that carried weight, and that I was just a person to help fill their quota of employees of a visible minority. At this time I was living in Mission, BC and decided that I wanted to move to Vancouver. I was presented with a job posting and applied to the public: untitled *project.*

When I started working for collective echoes, *I would barely participate in meetings, always had to be told what job had to be done next and had low self-esteem. I didn't participate because I was used to being shut down constantly, and I sadly accepted into my heart that people just didn't listen no matter in what capacity I spoke. I did not realise this about myself at the time, however, because the constant ignorance and abuse made me subconsciously shut down and close up to the world. I have been employed for a year, and it is amazing how much I have grown personally and professionally. I now take part in meetings, and have gained many skills including facilitation, mediation, book-keeping, project management, conflict resolution and public speaking. I also have the ability to speak my mind, and the self-esteem to let people know when they are shutting me down. I also have the awareness to realise when I am shutting other people down.*

Conflicts and problems still happen while working at collective echoes, *but every workplace has its problems because we are only human. However, this is the first place I've been where everyone takes responsibility for their actions and where there is space to speak when there has been wrong done. I know that the people here are interested in what I have to say and that I do have a voice that carries weight. The difference here is that we each take the time to apologise for our mistakes as well as thank the person for pointing it out. People cannot learn from their mistakes if they don't realise that they are making them. This is a policy that I feel every workplace should uphold. I am honoured to be working in such an environment where I can be me and am comfortable around my peers.*

As a final note I would also like to add that when someone asks me my nationality, I now say 'I am First Nations … and part Italian'.

Case Study 3

A Study Visit to Malawi

Stephen Adjei, *Connect Youth International*

Connect Youth aims to enhance the reputation of the United Kingdom in the world as a valued partner, and to further the personal and social education of young people in the UK.

Connect Youth runs programmes that give young people international experience. We believe that bringing young people together lets them learn about each other and teaches them more about themselves. Our programmes are open to everybody; there are no entry qualifications people have to meet before they can take part. We target young people who do not normally have the chance to go abroad.

We are the UK's national agency for the European Commission's Youth Programme and are active in the following areas:

- Youth Exchanges
- European Voluntary Service
- Group Initiatives
- Future Capital
- British Council Youth Millennium Awards.

Connect Youth International supports a regional network of 12 committees giving advice and support locally. Their responsibilities include the selection of projects and awarding of grants.

Project description

Connect Youth wishes to contribute to the world debate on youth empowerment and youth participation. To broaden our understanding of the global context of this debate, we organised a visit to Malawi, Africa, in February, 2001. This was a follow-up to a study visit conducted in 1999.

Visit to Area 25 Youth Office, Youdaos, Lilongwe

The Youth Development and Advancement Organisation is an NGO started in 1997 by post-primary school leavers as a youth group. It was established to enhance youth participation in social, political and economic development through education and training. The organisation currently runs the following programmes:

- Campaign on HIV/AIDS

- Environmental Management
- Youth Reproductive Health
- Youth Participation Programme

The Environmental Management Programme aims to reduce deforestation by planting trees and manufacturing fuel briquettes which are used by families for cooking, as a substitute for firewood. The Youth Reproductive Health programme focuses on school-going youth, and deals with issues of sexual health and adolescent development. The Youth Participation Programme mainly works by mobilising young people into clubs and groups.

I was informed by the manager of the Centre that UNICEF had provided funding on two separate occasions to support the centre's programmes. However, it was clear that there were some young people in the community who could not be accessed due to lack of resources. The Centre runs a number of clubs in school and out of school. The School Clubs Programme is being managed in partnership with head teachers who act as patrons for the clubs.

Visit to Centre for Youth and Children's Affairs (CEYCA), Lilongwe

The Centre for Youth and Children Affairs runs 21 youth clubs, and targets out-of-school youth. It provides counselling and other services to clubs within the community. The programme focuses on the economic empowerment of young people. The manager explained that they were trying to incorporate school-going youth as well. In 1999, CEYCA established the first youth centre within a traditional authority area. The centre also runs a youth initiative programme. It provides assistance to young people who decide to establish their own business such as poultry farming and marketing. However, the Centre faces a number of challenges, including lack of funds, resources, and skilled and professional staff.

Visit to Youth Net and Counselling (YONECO), Zomba

Youth Net and Counselling (YONECO) was founded in September 1997 as an NGO. It is a non-political and non-profit making centre, and is registered under the Trustees Incorporation Act (1962) of Malawi.

Mission statement:

- *To create a body of youth that is normally healthy and appreciates the need to exercise human rights in a responsible manner realising also the needs of others.*
- *To make young person realise his/her role in their own growth and development*
- *To give the youth skills to live in a self-reliant manner, knowing where to seek advice and what kind of advice to seek*

- *To fill gaps of essential services vis à vis sound youth development.*

The following are the objectives:

- To provide the youth with access to appropriately balanced information and knowledge about democracy and human rights;

- To promote and safeguard human rights and, in particular, child rights;

- To stimulate political thinking, evolution and participation in young people;

- To promote respect for and protection of the rights of children in a partici-patory manner.

The Centre has trained a number of youth workers who are engaged in the following programmes.

Drug Demand Reduction (DDR): The Centre runs a youth-friendly programme known as Drug Demand Reduction. Voluntary youth workers operate in partnership with the police to arrest drug suppliers. Many young people are using marijuana because traditionally it is used for medicinal purposes. For instance, they have seen their parents use it for various cures, including the cure of measles. It has, therefore, been difficult to persuade young people to stop using drugs as they often find the message confusing. The Centre is using peer education to raise awareness, and to explain the dangers in using drugs, among young people within the community.

Street Kids/Homelessness: There are many orphans living on the streets, and detached youth workers work with young people on the streets, offering them counselling services and support. The Centre currently houses 15 homeless kids, and is looking for resources to expand the programme. When I asked why the young people are willing to use a very basic facility at the Centre, I was told that the Centre is their only hope and the young people have great trust in the staff.

The challenges facing the centre are lack of resources, money, and skilled and professional staff.

Visit to Active Youth Initiative for Social Enhancement (AYISE), Blantyre

AYISE is a non-partisan, non-profit making voluntary organisation based in a suburb of Blantyre. It was established by young people in October 1995.

AYISE's eight main objectives are the following:

- Provision of Youth Reproductive Health Services

- Talent Promotion and Career Guidance

- Environmental Protection, Conservation and Rehabilitation

- Youth Economic Empowerment

- Promotion and Protection of Human Rights and Democratic Principles

- Conflict Prevention and Promotion of Unity

- Civic Education

- Grassroots Infrastructural Development through the concept of workcamps.

The organisation has been conducting human rights and democracy awareness meetings. It is also involved in peer education, training, advocacy, reproductive health lectures for school-going and out-of-school youth, and counselling. The Manager of AYISE said the Centre runs a youth-friendly project with the local hospital. She explained that this was necessary because young people in Blantyre have developed their own jargon to describe their illnesses – the result of their concern for confidentiality. There were instances where young people have been turned away by doctors or nurses who did not understand the terms being used by young people.

AYISE has designed a confidential hospital form for use by young people. When young people visit the centre, staff assist them in completing the medical forms by describing their illness in plain, ordinary English. This helps to avoid misunderstandings when they visit the hospital. According to the manager, the reason many young people frequent the Centre today, is the absolute trust established between staff and young people, and the staff's ability to understand youth language. This system makes it possible for more young people in Blantyre area to benefit from the medical facilities without going through interrogations by doctors and nurses.

Visit to Zingawa Youth Centre

This Centre is situated in an economically deprived area of Blantyre. It provides library services to over 3000 young people. The Centre has plans to offer training in marketing, farming, poultry etc. The Manager explained that when young people have designed a programme, they are sometimes forced to shelve the plan because donor agencies are not prepared to provide funding.

Other challenges facing the centre include a shortage of professional staff, and a lack of recreational facilities.

Outcomes of the Visit: Lessons and Future Action

The visit was rewarding and gave me the opportunity to visit a broad selection of organisations dealing with youth issues. In Malawi, youth structures are firmly in place. However, most of the centres lack funding and other vital resources.

It was felt by youth leaders in Malawi that one of the problems they were facing in running their youth organisations was lack of leadership skills. Connect Youth therefore committed itself to support a youth workers' training programme. We have since funded youth leadership training in Malawi.

The trip was tiring sometimes, but always enjoyable and educative. On behalf of Connect Youth International, I would like to express my sincere thanks to Mr Alex Mseka and his team for organising the visit.

Case study 4

On the EDGE

A desire to engage past participants of Canada World Youth leads to a dynamic, capable and respected youth organisation.

Canada World Youth (CWY) is a national non-governmental organisation that provides young people from Canada and around the world with the opportunity to travel, live and work in different communities, to learn about local and international development, and to gain important job skills for the future. Founded in 1971 by the Hon. Jacques Hébert, retired Senator and well-known Canadian writer and publisher, CWY programmes operate in Africa, Asia, Latin America and the Caribbean, and Central and Eastern Europe. More than 26,000 young people from Canada and abroad have participated in Canada World Youth; approximately 1,000 young people participate annually, more than 600 of whom are Canadians. Participants are recruited through five regional offices in British Columbia, Prairies, Ontario, Quebec and Atlantic.

Education and Development in a Global Environment (EDGE) is an Atlantic association of past participants of CWY programmes and other young people who are interested in social justice, environment and development issues. Created in 1994, EDGE is based in the Atlantic Regional Office of CWY, and receives organisational support in the form of a paid, part-time co-ordinator (five hours a week) during the school year, which becomes a full-time position during the summer months. The co-ordinator works from the Atlantic Regional Office, with dedicated office space and support.

The EDGE initiative

EDGE was not conceived as a 'project' with a finite end-date nor with specific objectives. It was —and is — an evolving relationship between Canada World Youth and youth who have participated in its education programmes.

EDGE mandate

- To provide a volunteer base to work with the Canada World Youth (CWY) Atlantic Regional Office, providing support to Atlantic programmes and promoting public awareness of CWY

- To promote continued learning and skills development of members through their involvement in EDGE and to provide a means for social interaction and contact among past participants and volunteers

- To promote international and community development education activities in Atlantic Canada and other regions, and participate in projects focused on social and environmental justice.

Origins of EDGE

Past participants of CWY programmes have always been involved with the Atlantic Regional Office (ARO) as volunteers. Over time it became apparent that common interests could be served if these past participants and volunteers were given sufficient support to initiate the formation of a new organisation. EDGE was born as the result of an ARO decision to commit funds for a five-hour-per-week position of EDGE Co-ordinator. Essentially the decision to provide that support came from recognition of an untapped youth-based resource, whereby the ARO could engage youth in a post-programme period, thus extending the relationship between CWY and its past participants. With the support of federal and provincial job-creation grants, the Co-ordinator position becomes a full-time job during the summer months. The EDGE co-ordinator is provided with access to a computer, communications (fax, e-mail, phone) and all the benefits of being located in an office. The ARO also allocates some staff time to be responsible for support to EDGE, including occasional attendance at group meetings and the role of support person.

Projects and activities

EDGE draws upon the dynamism and energy of its youth membership to undertake projects and initiatives that are relevant to its mandate. While the EDGE Co-ordinator's salary is covered by the ARO and the summer student-job programme, the organisation has a small annual budget. It undertakes revenue-generation through fundraising events, such as public showings of the EcoEgypt video, honoraria from workshop presentations,such as CWY's pre-departure and follow-up sessions with participants, and with the Rural Youth Education Project, and occasional additional support from the ARO when budgets permit. Some of EDGE's activities are:

- EDGE worked in partnership with CWY and the Arab Office for Youth and Environment on Eco-Egypt '98, a project promoting sustainable tourism in Egypt. The youth participants produced a documentary video and accompanying website, 'Beyond Pyramids: Exploring EcoTourism in Egypt' (http://chebucto.ca/~ecoegypt). The video was officially presented at a United Nations NGO Forum of the Commission on Sustainable Development in New York in April, 1999. The project was made possible with the financial support of the International Development Research Centre (IDRC), CWY and the National Film Board (NFB).

- EDGE has been involved with the Nova Scotia Environmental Networks Youth Caucus Steering Committee and is an active participant in Oxfam-Halifax's Globalization Working Group.

- With funding from the Canadian International Development Agency (CIDA) Development Information Programme (DIP), EDGE prepared print media articles and media training on 'Co-operating for the Earth', based on a CWY environmental project in Costa Rica (summer 2000–spring 2001).

- The relationship between environment and development continued to be explored in another EDGE effort, its participation in the UN Commission on Sustainable Development initiative on sustainable tourism. Working with other youth organisations, EDGE intends to present a 'Global Youth Charter for Sustainable Tourism' at the third U. Earth Summit in 2002, the International Year of EcoTourism.

- EDGE presented a workshop on 'Building Cross-Cultural Bridges' at the National Youth Summit, on Prince Edward Island in April 2001, organised by the Coalition of National Voluntary Organizations. as part of activities for the UN International Year of the Volunteer.

- EDGE is a partner in the Rural Youth Education Project (RYEP), a development education workshop series for youth in rural high schools across Nova Scotia. Their workshops cover issues of globalisation, based on the CCIC model.

- EDGE publishes a seasonal newsletter, *Letters from the EDGE*, which includes articles from past participants on their CWY experiences, articles on development, social justice, environment and youth empowerment, upcoming events, international and community resources, and more.

- EDGE organises an annual youth retreat weekend every fall, which includes skills workshops, sessions on development issues, project planning, and a fun, relaxed time for members to meet and re-connect with each other. A vital component of sustainability within a development-education/social justice-action organisation such as EDGE is the internal prominence given to awareness of the issues and democratic process. The annual retreat activities help to provide this.

- EDGE volunteers represent CWY at public events and high schools, and support CWY in pre-departure and post-programme activities with participants.

Youth participation

Consistent with the CWY mission to increase the ability of people, and especially young people, to actively engage in the development of just, harmonious and sustainable societies, the decision by the ARO to support past participants provided the vital support structure to launch EDGE. With a paid position and office resources, EDGE was able to stay 'in the loop' with CWY regional activities. It is important to note that CWY created the conditions in which EDGE could do its own thing; the EDGE membership chooses the person to fill the position of co-ordinator during the school year. The CWY Programme Officer provides support, but acts in a consultative manner, not directive or supervisory. The relationship is one of mentorship, and of encouragement. EDGE is in all respects its own organisation.

With regard to the ongoing EDGE/ARO relationship, 'mutually beneficial' remains an apt description, six years after the creation of this youth organisation.

Achievements

To say that EDGE has been successful in meeting its mandate would be an understatement. In terms of the support EDGE provides to CWY, the group's members volunteer to represent CWY when delivering skills-development presentations at high schools across the region. In collaboration with CWY, they provide a peer-organised, fun follow-up gathering for participants newly returned from CWY programmes. In this way, EDGE provides past participants with a vehicle for moving on to the next stage in their lives. For many, this means becoming involved in development education in their own communities. A large number of former CWY participants use the Youth Exchange Programme as a 'break' between high school and college, and find themselves drawn to programmes of international development or environment. EDGE exists in a similar fashion to serve as a bridge for participants between their overseas experience and involvement in NGOs in the development community. Within EDGE, members pursue projects consistent with the organisation's mandate and their individual interests.

Challenges and reflections

Considering the nature of the membership of EDGE, it is not surprising that one challenge is in the turnover of the members. Youth in this age group (late teens to mid-20s) are heading to university, pursuing additional overseas experiences, and in general are less likely to be tied down to one physical location. This has been true with EDGE, which has countered that tendency with effective recruitment of past participants on an annual basis and the integration of new members.

Another issue is the location of EDGE in Halifax, while having the entire Atlantic region as its service area. CWY participants are drawn from diverse geographic locations, which places added communication and participation difficulties on EDGE activities. To maintain an informative and consultative nature, EDGE makes efficient use of e-mail and distributes *Letters from the EDGE*. EDGE has set up a structure that welcomes and encourages new members and is guided by a mission that is constant and relevant to the membership's interests.

EDGE is a small youth organisation which has done remarkable things. It has garnered a reputation for being highly active and very capable, and has recently been recognised at a local level with the award of the YMCA Peace Medal and at the national level with the award of the Arthur Kroeger College of Public Affairs Citizenship Award. Now in its sixth year, EDGE is in the enviable position of having to 'live up to itself'.

This initiative by the ARO – to support past participants in their desire to organise around common interests and activities – has resulted in an organic, vibrant and successful collaboration. Canada World Youth envisions a world of active, engaged global citizens who share responsibility for the well-being of all people and the planet. Members of EDGE embody the qualities and passions of global citizens of today and tomorrow.

Case Study 5

Youth Participation in the International Planned Parenthood Federation*

Kathryn M Faulkner and Jessica Nott

The International Planned Parenthood Federation (IPPF) is the world's largest voluntary organisation in the field of sexual and reproductive health and rights, including family planning. It works in over 180 countries worldwide. As a Federation, IPPF works at the international and regional level and through Family Planning Associations (FPAs) at a local level. At the international and regional level, IPPF runs a secretariat to share information between the different regions and FPAs, and to promote sexual and reproductive health issues.

IPPF has a long history of working with young people at the grassroots. Efforts have also been made to integrate young people's views in work at the international level for almost a quarter of a century. These efforts have moved from sporadic international youth consultation meetings and collaborative youth projects to more systematic consultation with young people through the IPPF youth committee – an advisory body on policy issues for the Federation. In 1998, during the restructuring of IPPF's highest decision-making body, it was decided that 20 per cent of the Governing Council would be young people under the age of 25 years. This groundbreaking move demonstrates IPPF's commitment to youth participation. It is just one part of a process to institutionalise the participation of young people at all levels of the Federation, and has created the impetus for the development of a dynamic network of young people working on sexual and reproductive health issues. Needless to say, this is a process that has only just begun, and there are many lessons to be learned along the way.

This process has forced IPPF to look critically at its own structures and decision-making mechanisms as well as its approach to young people. In November 2000, an IPPF was held with 12 young people from around the world and staff from each of the six regions. The working group came together to appraise IPPF's approach to youth participation, to reflect on how far IPPF has come and to look for ways forward.

---

*The concepts and ideas expressed in this case study are based on the work of the following people who attended the IPPF Youth Working Group meeting in November 2000: Roellya Ardhyaning Tyas; Kofi Boakye Dankwa; Doortje Braeken; Mijail Garvich Claux; Edith Yanira Cruz; Gill Gordon, Reproductive Health Alliance Europe; Naomi Imani; Catherine Kamau; Namit Kapoor; Radhia Kour; Roni Liyanage; Velimira Atanossova Mladenova; Imtiaz Mohammed; Zaina Nyiramatama; Kolbrun Palsdottir; Christopher Penales; Zakieh Shirafkan; Chokri Ben Yahia.

IPPF Youth Working Group Meeting, November 2000
Rationale behind the participation of young people in IPPF

It is really nice to know that you have something to give and that you are worthwhile for the world.

Roellya Ardhyaning Tyas, Youth Volunteer, Indonesia

Allowing young people to make their own choices about relationships and sex has long been perceived by IPPF as their right. If it is accepted that young people should be able to make their own decisions about their personal lives, then by extension they should be involved in programmes and processes that affect their lives. Believing that young people have the right to participate is part of a philosophy that respects their ability to make informed decisions.

Yet young people are regularly denied this opportunity or, at best, are given very constricted opportunities. Why is this? One of the answers to this question has its roots in traditional ways of thinking about childhood and adolescence. This model treats young people as immature and irrational (Boyden, 1997). By definition, young people's views under a certain age can be considered 'childish', making it easier for adults to dismiss them if they wish. Another reason for treating young people as dependent, passive recipients could be that adults can reinforce their monopoly of power. In the sensitive area of sexuality, adults, who are also parents, may feel threatened.

Participation is not a luxury. Excluding young people from participating in decisions deprives them of crucial opportunities for personal growth and socialisation, and ignores their wide range of experience and expertise.

Exploring different perceptions of participation

Participation means paying attention to each individual opinion ... one person does not know everything so we should all work together.

Kofi Boakye Dankwa, IPPF Youth Working Group Member, Ghana

- Participation means so many things to so many people, but what does 'participation' mean to the young people taking part in IPPF's meetings?

- Is 'participation' of a young person as a peer educator in a local sexual health clinic the same as 'participation' on a board of an international organisation?

Exploring young people's definitions and experiences of participation is an important prerequisite to establishing how young people can most effectively participate. The IPPF Youth Working Group looked at the different ways they perceived their own and other young people's participation (see Box 1).

Box 1

Participation is:

1. A right
- Being part of decision making
- Not being spoken *about* but speaking *with*
- Having a sense of ownership
- Being treated as equal partners
- Being really listened to
- Having a voice
- Making sure that projects reflect what young people really want
- Being actively involved
- Being part of wider processes.

2. Being a team
- Mutual empowerment
- Using individual talent for the collective benefit of the team
- Equal partners
- Acknowledging and respecting differences
- Having a choice
- Co-ordinating and co-operation
- Respecting all members
- Not expecting awards
- Passing investment and experience to others.

3. Democracy
- Representation
- Being accountable/ensuring accountability
- Effective communication
- Information
- Having a role and knowing why you are participating
- Equal opportunities to participate
- Being able to set the agenda
- Being able to make mistakes
- Expressing ideas in the way you want.

4. Personal
- Being able to challenge
- Not being afraid to speak.

Participation is *not*:
- Having to become 'adult' like
- Having to know everything.

Participants worked in groups, exchanging personal experiences of positive and negative participation, and drawing on their personal experiences of volunteering at various levels of the Federation. These were presented as a series of role plays. Boxes 2 and 3 show the results of these role plays.

Box 2. Positive experiences of participation

1. Flexible adults and people in authority

2. When young people
   a. Are assertive
   b. Have training
   c. Speak out about problems
   d. Do not give up easily
   e. Learn from each other
   f. Are prepared. This means they need to have access to all necessary information

3. Support from other young people and adults

4. Involving young people in evaluating their own participation

5. Persuasiveness
   a. Using passionate language
   b. Starting with less controversial things

6. Fitting in with organisational objectives
   a. Having a clear role

7. Keeping a clear and cool head

8. An atmosphere that is
   a. Informal and relaxed
   b. Time is given for people to talk and ask questions one-to-one

9. Young people can learn things from participating in seminars and meetings

10. Young people are able to set the agenda

11. Participation should be continuous
    a. It is important to follow up meetings
    b. It is important to get evaluations of participation from young people and act on them

---

Box 3 Negative experiences of participation

1. Lack of information
   a. Young people are not given basic information, especially on organisational structures and programmes
   b. Outcomes of youth meetings are not reported back to young people

2. Not having a voice
   a. At meetings young people are not always listened to or asked about their views
   b. Young people are unable to determine the outcomes

3. Lack of communication
   a. Young people may not be asked questions because they are either: intimidated, patronised or talked at

4. Inequality (hierarchy is bad)
   a. Young people's views are dismissed
   b. Unable to challenge people in powerful positions
   c. Even though young people might have the same status as older people, they may still be treated differently

5. Exploitation
   a. Young people's ideas can be used by others with no recognition
   b. Young people can be blamed if things go wrong
   c. Young people can be given pointless tasks

6. Specific situations problems
   a. Individuals can be obstructive
   b. Different organisations work in different ways

7. Staff can lack responsibility for young people
   a. Staff may note willing to work in partnership with young people
   b. Staff can be inflexible and don't make time for young people
   c. Staff do not always give personal support

8. High turnover of young people

9. Lack of continuity and follow-up of different participatory processes

Adapted from 2nd Youth Working Group Report, IPPF , November 2000

Practical ways forward

I say congratulations, but I must say there is more room for improvement.
                    Kofi Boakye Dankwa, IPPF Youth Working Group member, Ghana

Participants identified some crucial issues that need development to move forward with the idea of youth participation in IPPF.

1. Strengthening IPPF's network of young people at the local, regional and international levels through creation of a youth database, listserv and website. Also establishing regional youth working groups.

2. Establishing election procedures for young people on regional and governing councils.

3. Integrating young people into further areas of IPPF's work, and consulting more widely with young people on proposals, publications, evaluations and situation analysis.

4. Investing in young staff members, encouraging departments to recruit young staff and involving young people on job interview panels.

5. Establishing youth focal points and, through them, establishing a strong network of young people.

Training is crucial for supporting and sustaining young people's participation. Suggested training areas include management of youth groups, project-writing and monitoring, using the media, budgeting, as well as personal development skills such as public speaking and confidence-building exercises. Training is also vital for staff and older members so that they can truly understand, value and support young people's participation. Another important area is ensuring that experiences are passed on – not only between generations, but among young people themselves.

Outcomes: lessons learned about participation

Participation is about choices. The first choice is whether or not to participate. This requires providing young people with full information about what the expected outcome is, and what their role and position would be within the task. Young people should not be included simply because it looks good for an organisation, but because their opinions are valued and the choices and decisions they make are respected

Like all people, young people sometimes make mistakes. Bringing young people into new arenas that have previously been closed to them makes the likelihood of mistakes higher. It is through these mistakes that learning happens. Such mistakes might also prompt an organisation to look at its own structures and procedures critically, and to make them more supportive. Too often at the international level, ideas are expressed in difficult jargon. There should be no pressure on young people to adapt their language and behaviour to fit in with over-complex or restrictive concepts. An environment needs to be created in which everyone feels able to contribute, and in which young people are not afraid to speak.

Issues of representation raise another set of challenges. To what extent should young people be required to participate as representatives of other young people

– and whom are they actually representing? This is not just a personal issue, it is also a question for the organisation to consider. Within IPPF, we are still trying to devise effective structures to enable young people to democratically select young representatives to the Governing Council. One idea, which is yet to be implemented, is to set up local and regional networks of young people who can feed their ideas to their regional youth representatives on the Governing Council, and from whom the representatives would get their mandate.

Another issue is who comes forward as a representative or volunteer. Many young people may be ruled out because they lack the time and resources needed to attend international meetings. For those young people who work, time constraints pose particular difficulties; many volunteers at the international level tend to be students. Issues of language pose other barriers, especially where translation cannot be provided. For these reasons volunteers tend to be well-off, well-educated and articulate, with good spoken English.

With representation comes the issue of accountability. Adults who attend meetings, sit on boards and participate in activities are rarely asked to make statements on behalf of all adults; yet the pressure on young people to speak on behalf of all young people is tremendous. We need to value young people for their own experiences and contributions, and support them to link up with others – not pressure them to speak on behalf of all their peers. And to do this, as well as to keep in touch with what is going on within the organisation, they need access to communication channels such as internet, telephone and fax.

Adults need to be prepared to relinquish power to young people and allow them to take a full part in proceedings, including being able to set the agenda. Questions need to be asked about how young people can participate, what roles they will take on, and what kind of shifts in the power dynamics are needed for genuine and meaningful participation of young people. Organisations must be prepared to question their whole way of working – with the result that the organisation itself will need to change and adapt if it is to deliver on its commitment to meaningful youth participation.

We don't only form part of the problem, we are able to make decisions and we can help in finding solutions that are concrete and real.

Claudia Montalvo Sánchez, youth volunteer, Peru

References

Boyden, J. (1997). 'Childhood and Policymakers: A Comparative Perspective on the Globalisation of Childhood' in: James, A. and Prout, A., eds. *Constructing and reconstructing childhood: contemporary issues in the sociological study of childhood.* Falmer Press: London

IPPF (1998). Youth Manifesto.

IPPF (nd). 1st Youth Working Group report.

IPPF (nd). 2nd Youth working group report.

Case Study 6

Bluepeace: Conservation in the Maldives

Hassan Shifau

Bluepeace is the only NGO in the Maldives to be founded, led and driven by young people. It is totally dedicated to sustainable development. The name Bluepeace reflects the colour of our environment: Maldives is 99 per cent sea, and the sky is blue also. As Maldivians – children of the sea – our survival, livelihood, culture and traditions are linked to the sea. Even our dry land is given by the sea. The reefs produce sand, which collects and forms islands, and the reefs ensure the protection of those islands from ocean currents and waves.

Realising the delicate nature of our ecosystem and its socio-economic importance, a group of young people got together in September 1989 and decided to make a difference. Hence, Bluepeace was born with the objectives of:

• Creating environmental awareness among the public;

• Co-operating with national and international organisations in all their efforts to conserve and protect the environment;

• Initiating and implementing environmental activities and projects at various levels in the Maldives;

• Securing resources and expertise for environmental protection and conservation efforts.

Bluepeace implements its sustainable environmental development agenda through activities such as awareness campaigns, grassroots workshops, lectures for students, mass media reporting, publications, marking of events and days, clean-up campaigns, and participation in national events in collaboration with government and other NGOs. All ideas and activism generated from Bluepeace are expressions of young people, who are well represented on the Board of Directors as well as the membership.

The threat of extinction of marine turtles

Maldives has a very rich tropical marine environment and is a habitat for a host of tropical fish, corals and thousands of other marine dwellers. Also, being an archipelago it is endowed with white sandy beaches providing nesting grounds for at least five species of marine turtles listed as endangered.

Marine turtles are fascinating reptiles that have lived on Earth for over one hundred million years. Their primordial and peculiar nesting habits and low survival rate have brought them close to extinction. Trading of turtle parts has been banned, as recorded in Appendix 1 of the Convention on International Trade in Endangered Species of Wild Fauna and Flora (CITES).

Marine turtles are great voyagers, relying on the earth's magnetic field and wave motion for guidance. They travel long distances and across oceans over many years and accurately track their way back to their birthplace for nesting.

Maldives has a long history of marine turtle-hunting for meat, and poaching of eggs for exotic dishes. However, the total stock of turtle population was long undisturbed due to the availability of a number of virgin nesting habitats and abundance of food. Then, marine turtle shell became the fastest moving product in souvenirs for the growing tourist industry. Young people with and around Bluepeace became increasingly concerned that marine turtles in the Maldives were being over-exploited and were on the verge of extinction.

Maldives was once a haven for turtles to nest and breed, but due to human intervention and greed, nature's balance was disrupted. By the 1990s, the over-exploitation had peaked to the extent that there was hardly any reporting on turtle sighting by nature-lovers and scuba divers. Around the world, the survival rate of marine turtles reached less than 1 per cent due to continued turtle-hunting for commercial needs, complemented by other threats such as marine pollution, accidentally getting caught in nets and hooks, turtles accidentally consuming synthetic material, predators, beach and soil erosion, and artificial development of coastal areas for tourism.

Campaign strategies developed and implemented by young people

Bluepeace reacted to the situation by formulating the 'Marine Turtle Conservation Campaign'. The group targeted the public through mass media campaigns and lobbied the government to bring out rules to restrict turtle-hunting and poaching of eggs. The campaign was launched in January 1990 by distributing greeting cards with the slogan 'SOS Marine Turtles! – Save Marine Turtles' to senior government dignitaries, public figures and businessmen. Bluepeace has a tradition of assigning a theme for every year and focusing its efforts on the theme. But in the case of turtle conservation, it continued for three consecutive years. To generate publicity, we printed and distributed T-shirts and stickers with slogans on turtle conservation. As a major component of the project, we started research on marine turtles, their life-cycle, migratory patterns and their habitats in the Maldives. At the same time, we initiated an awareness and education campaign for students in the form of mini-lectures, and involved them in the information dissemination process by peer education. The Marine Turtle Conservation Campaign was designed in such a way that it had a 'multiplier' effect with information being passed on from friends to neighbours. This proved to be an inexpensive, yet high-impact technique. It allowed us to reach out to the most elusive target groups with our message. The impact of these messages delivered emotionally by children to their parents was greater than that through any other media.

Forging links

In 1992, one of our Executive Committee members called on His Excellency Maumoon Abdul Gayyoom, the President of Maldives, to bring to his notice our environmental concerns, especially that of turtle conservation. We also had the opportunity to take our message to various national and international forums on the environment.

While Bluepeace continued its research and awareness campaign, several NGOs joined the campaign and even took very radical stands. Our research work recommended the setting-up of a turtle hatchery in the Maldives. However, further research, and a subsequent study tour to a turtle hatchery based in Sri Lanka, contradicted our initial faith in artificial nurturing. We found that artificial nurturing tampers with the unique life cycle of marine turtles. The nesting, growth and survival of these creatures is linked to environmental conditions such as temperature, humidity and natural lighting. For example, the sex of the hatchling is determined by the weather conditions of the nest, and its travel from the nest to the sea is also determined by the natural composition of moonlight and its reflection on the sea. When reared at a hatchery, marine turtles' natural feeding habits and buoyancy controls are lost. Thus, the artificially reared young ones lack survival skills, have underdeveloped natural instincts, are unfit for living in the wilderness and are often easy prey for predators. Bluepeace immediately dropped the turtle hatchery project and continued the mass awareness campaign for the sustainable revival of turtle stock in the Maldives and the sustainable exploitation for exotic turtle meat. Therefore, Bluepeace started promoting natural turtle sanctuaries on certain uninhabited islands as an alternative to the development of hatcheries. These sanctuaries would be zones where people's activities against marine turtles would be restricted, and would be officially protected by the government.

We met with many business owners, especially those from the tourism industry, and informed and advised them of the importance of adhering to the eco-tourism and sustainable development concepts. We also advised them on ways to develop the beaches for tourists in a more turtle-friendly manner.

Meanwhile, the government had started taking necessary steps towards turtle conservation in the Maldives. Initially, a regulation was passed to ban hunting and catching of turtles less than a stipulated size. However, it was insufficient to make a positive impact as it still left eggs, as well as a portion of the productive adult population, unprotected. Further awareness and media reporting continued before the government imposed, in 1995, a more comprehensive moratorium of 10 years on turtle shell products, and declared protected zones and islands to facilitate natural sanctuaries. This achieved part of the short-term objective of the campaign, but the work continued as the revival of the turtle population in the

Maldives largely depended on the attitude of the people as well. In 1998, Bluepeace published a reference book on environmentally friendly lifestyles, which contributed to the turtle conservation project being launched into the academic arena; the book is widely used as a reference for environmental studies at lower secondary schools.

Outcomes of the campaign and future challenges

After eight years of government regulation of turtle hunting, the turtle population has started to flourish tremendously. The enormous amount of resources, time and effort pooled by many organisations and individuals had come to fruition. However, poaching of eggs still continues.

Looking back at the project – its conception, the long march and the success achieved – we realise that it was because of the coming together of like-minded young people full of energy, and with common objective and targets. A good deal of the campaign's success depended on our ability to tap into similar energy in our peers and the larger population. By involving young people in a participatory manner and making the young feel that they are an important part of a larger social structure, we proved that young people, if united, can make a positive difference to socio-economic and environmental development. There is no magic in the recipe but the lesson is that ideas need to evolve and radiate from young people themselves. The young have to internalise, believe and own the mission before their youthful energy can yield. At Bluepeace we believe that small, practical things can be put together for a greater and long-lasting impact. Minor activities such as producing T-shirts and stickers with turtle-conservation slogans had far greater impact than we ever expected.

Bluepeace does not attribute all the success of the mass campaign to itself. Credit is due to young people who concentrated their efforts and resources towards a common goal, the other NGOs who collaborated in the effort, and the government the Maldives for realising the importance of conserving and preserving our natural heritage and inheritance. The government responded positively to the plea and the expressions of the young citizens of the nation.

Now the challenge for Bluepeace is to educate the masses on the importance of sustaining the success achieved. There are a number of environmental threats and concerns that directly or indirectly affect the turtle population around the globe, and therefore, need to be addressed internationally. Bluepeace strongly recommends the establishing of a regional and international sea turtle conservation network to sustain the success of the Maldives and revive the sea turtle population around the globe. Sea turtles are migratory, and only regional and international collaboration will ensure safe passage for their long journeys on earth and to the future. In the Maldives we have proved that young people can make a difference. We need to prove this internationally.

Case Study 7
Pachen Village Water Supply Project

National Youth Movement Programme of Papua New Guinea

The Youth Pioneers Scheme (YPS) of the National Youth Movement Programme (NYMP) of Papua New Guinea has had a profound impact on communities that took part. One such community was the village of Pachen in the Yangoru area of the East Sepik Province. With encouragement, advice and assistance provided through the scheme, the Husena Youth group from Pachen completed a water supply project in the village. The success of the project over the past seven years is testimony to the positive transformation which a youth scheme such as the YPS can have on entire communities.

The YPS was a programme component of the NYMP. The scheme was initially introduced in 1984 through the Department of Home Affairs, in order to meaningfully involve Papua New Guinea's young people in the development of their communities.

The specific objectives of the programme were to:

- mobilise and enable youth to undertake community infrastructure projects;
- provide skill, discipline and citizenship training to the youth;
- involve youth in the development process of the nation, and
- promote national integration and nationalism.

Project identification and documentation

The scheme required community groups to identify the kind of training or service projects that were needed in their area. These were then documented as a project and forwarded to the Provincial Youth Council for appraisal and endorsement, and to the National Youth Co-ordinating Committee for funding considerations. Documentation was done by skilled resource people within the local area or sought from technical agencies of the government. Applications that were not identified with the consensus of the people were discouraged.

Funding of Projects: Funding was normally provided through a grant from the youth office, from other departments carrying out similar activities or through a donor agency. If approved, funds were channelled to the Provincial Youth Councils, so they could manage and disburse them to the approved projects. Wages or cash payments to young people were discouraged. Instead, funding was directed towards the purchase of materials needed for the projects, which were then supplied by the project committee.

Equity contribution: All community groups who applied for assistance under the project were encouraged to provide evidence of equity contribution. This could either be in cash or kind. Contributions were also sought from public institutions and individuals (provincial administrations, members of parliament etc.). Projects that did not have equity contributions were discouraged.

Training: All projects were encouraged to provide training to youth who would be employed in the project. The training normally consisted of leadership, citizenship and skills training related to the project. In cases where skills training could not be provided separately, training was done on the job as part of the project.

Project management: Project proponents were required to establish a co-ordinating committee, whose primary role would be to co-ordinate the community's participation in the training and projects. Duties included the selection of young participants, scheduling of youth work parties, fundraising, negotiating with the technical supervisory team, bringing out periodic progress and expenditure reports, and settling disputes.

Technical supervision: Each project was required to have a competent technical supervisor (such as a trained engineer or experienced builder). The technical supervisor, together with skilled youth, formed a technical core group for the proposed projects.

Roles and responsibilities: In successfully implementing such a scheme on a nationwide level, it was important that the roles and responsibilities of all concerned parties be clearly outlined in the implementation guidelines. The table below provides a summary of these responsibilities at the four levels of decision-making and administration. These responsibilities relate primarily to the role of youth offices, youth councils, youth co-ordination committees and the youth groups.

National	Provincial	District	Community/Local
Set policy guidelines	Carry out awareness	Carry out awareness	Identification of
Mobilise funding	Mobilise youth	Facilitate	project
Publicise scheme	Train youth leaders	identification	Equity contribution
Monitor	Appraise projects	Facilitate	Selection of youth
implementation	Recommend	documentation	participants
Fund approved	proposals for	Recommend	Provide reports
projects	funding to NYCC	proposals to PYC	Participate in
	Manage approved	Monitor	projects
	grants	implementation	
	Co-ordinate		
	programme in		
	provinces		

Project description: The Pachen Village Water Supply Project

The Pachen experience has clearly demonstrated that youth can become a catalyst for wholesome changes within their communities.

The Husena Youth Group learned about the Youth Pioneer Scheme through its adviser, Mr. Damien Sengi. Mr Damien witnessed the scheme's assistance to three projects in the neighbouring district of Wewak in 1985: in the villages of Passam (school classrooms rehabilitation), Turubu (women's training centre) and Kremending (water supply). Inspired by the positive impact of these projects on the communities, the Husena Youth Group was formed and registered with the East Sepik Provincial Youth Council on 2 February 1986.

In the youth meetings that followed, the community was asked to identify needy areas in the village. Water supply was identified as the first community project to be undertaken by the youth, and the request was forwarded to the youth office. The youth leaders were advised to approach the Health Extension Officer in the subdistrict to investigate and document the project before it could be processed for funding considerations. The transfer of the Health Extension Officer to another district delayed the investigations until the matter was presented again in 1991.

Eventually, the request was given preliminary approval in 1992 by the East Sepik Rural Water Supply project. A detailed technical survey was carried out in 1992 and the design was formulated. In July 1994, the health extension officers and youth from the community constructed the water supply following a grant of Kina 15,000 ($US1 = K3.30) from the European Union's Rural Water Supply programme. It took three months and three days to complete. Youth and the community contributed K2000 in cash, and K4000 in kind to the project.

The project consisted of three kilometres of pipe-line, a water catchment box, and eight community taps. It cost approximately K7.00 per metre, including materials, labour and other project overheads. The total project cost in monetary terms was K21,000. The youth and the community raised their contributions by levying K20.00 per family and also collected 0.50t per youth. Those working away from the village sent in their contributions.

Youth leaders took charge of the village co-ordinating committee with elders as advisers. The committee co-ordinated the work parties and ensured the technical team was taken care of during their stay at the village. It ensured that all conflicts and problems were resolved during the entire period of construction. The project was completed without a hitch. The project is still operational and is maintained from fees collected within the community.

How the Youth Project transformed the community

The Pachen Village Water Supply project is just one example of how a good programme can meaningfully transform the lives of young people and their community. If the move towards strengthening youth participation is done by the community itself, and not imposed from outside, then such service projects are capable of changing a community's way of life.

Husena Youth Group's accomplishments have placed youth at the centre of decision-making in the village. Today, the youth are more confident in discussing community issues as well as national issues of concern to the village. For example, in village meetings, elders have made provisions for youth to voice their views. This is a significant change from past practice. Today the elders pay respect to youth leaders in community meetings.

Remarkably, a number of customary practices considered detrimental to the welfare of the village have been discarded upon the advice of the youth. For example, pigs used to be raised in the village for traditional rituals and exchange ceremonies. When it was pointed out that domesticating pigs required that fences be built around gardens, and that such intensive labour was taking its toll on people's health and keeping them from engaging in more important activities, the village substituted chickens for pigs.

Young people are now actively involved in the development process of the district. A radical change from the 'back-seat' or passive attitude of the past was evident in the last local government elections, when, with the support of the youth, the village was very successful in installing their candidate. In the coming national elections, the Husena Youth Group has requested a respected person from the village to contest. When this case study was being prepared, they were mobilising village people, including those in the neighbouring area, to support their potential candidate.

Husena youth will no doubt become a role model to youth groups in the Yangoru area of the East Sepik Province in terms of the confidence and the experience they have built up. Indeed, most rural youth do not need to be told what their needs are. They are well aware of them. They need to be provided the opportunity and guidance to prove their capabilities. If the government of Papua New Guinea is to address problems of rural youth and their communities, programmes such as the Youth Pioneer Scheme deserves high priority for funding.

Lessons learned from Pachen village

There are important lessons to be learned from the manner in which the Youth Pioneer Scheme was able to empower youth and 'mainstream' their participation in the development process of their community. The most notable outcomes of this scheme are discussed below:

Firstly, YPS allowed youth and their respective communities to decide their own priorities and needs. Upon reaching a consensus, they received guidance and encouragement through agents such as the community youth co-ordinators.

Secondly, it is essential to understand that young people everywhere want better lives for themselves. They have a lot of energy and are very adventurous. Thus, they are very willing to attempt anything that gives them a sense of satisfaction and self-esteem within their community. A scheme such as the YPS allows them to tap into their enormous potential and earns them respect from older members of their community.

Thirdly, not all young people need to have trade skills to contribute to the improvement of community infrastructures. They only need basic training and technical supervision from a competent supervisor to accomplish less complex projects. In many cases, there are already people in the local communities that have the basic skills to cope with the demands of projects such as community water supplies.

Fourthly, young people readily take on responsibility if they have a sense of ownership. This can only be possible if they are involved in the identification, planning and implementation of projects, and share the responsibility for the welfare of their communities.

Fifthly, it is important to understand that networking provides opportunities to enlist the support of agencies providing important services to the community. It is through this network that misconceptions about the abilities of youth can be dispelled. Young people must not be seen as a segregated segment of our population, as is typical of many Western approaches to youth development. Young people are an integral part of our families, community and development process.

Finally, the 'hand-out' mentality as seen in some welfare state or youth grants will only make youth a liability to the nation's development. Good programmes will encourage young people to find their place as productive members of communities by being involved in community development initiatives.

Case Study 8

World Assembly of Youth: Development of Youth and Population Handbook

Background to the project

The World Assembly of Youth (WAY) took note of the fact that the world population is rapidly increasing and posing grave concerns. The world population was 4 billion in 1976, by 1991 it was 5.5 billion, and by 2000 it had soared to 6 billion. The effects of population growth were visible all around the world: too few jobs, crowded schools, expanding cities, jammed roads, incapacitated health delivery systems, insufficient housing and a polluted environment.

The 12th General Assembly of the World Assembly of Youth resolved to tackle population issues seriously and mandated the Executive Committee and Secretariat to identify project opportunities that would contribute to the control of mounting population concerns. A proposal was developed, and in partnership with the United Nations Population Fund (UNFPA) WAY started to work on its Youth and Population Handbook.

Objectives of the Handbook project

The objectives of developing the Youth and Population Handbook were to:

- Raise awareness on the importance of population issues;
- Highlight current and future global population challenges;
- Educate young people on population growth and development issues;
- Highlight the need for family planning and safe motherhood;
- Discuss issues regarding sexuality and STDs;
- Develop a template for population project formulation;
- Indicate potential sources of resources for population projects;
- Identify action – steps needs to be taken by youth organisations.

The aim of the Youth and Population Handbook project was to produce a comprehensive, understandable, yet stimulating publication that young people at all levels, including grassroots, national, regional and global structures, could use.

Facilitating youth participation

It was clear from the inception that designing a handbook for young people needed the involvement of the young people themselves. WAY believes that the active participation of young people in population, health, development and environmental programmes is the best guarantee for the future. WAY has been active in population awareness programmes for young people since 1968, and considers population and family planning activities to be key components of development programmes. The Youth and Population Handbook project was considered one of the largest youth and population programmes ever conducted in co-operation with the UNFPA and the International Planned Parenthood Federation.

Young people were involved in all stages of the project. When the application for funding was made, it was on the basis of input received from young people about their areas of need. All the manpower and labour, whether voluntary or hired, was of people below the age of 40.

In preparation for the handbook, a questionnaire was circulated to samples of young people in three continents (Africa, Asia and Latin America). The responses helped to show the needs of the youth in terms of population planning.

Apart from making substantive contributions to the style and content of the handbook, young people were also involved in the project's decision-making and implementation. The Board of WAY is the main policy-maker and it consists of young people. The project co-ordinators, who were responsible for implementing the project, were hired young interns.

Project planning, execution and findings

A project team was formed, headed by the WAY Secretary-General. The team consisted of four additional staff from the WAY Secretariat, as well as a consultant in each region of the world. Once the division of responsibilities was completed, work began on the challenging but rewarding task of developing the Handbook.

The first step was to hold consultations around the world, obtaining youth perspectives on population issues, as well as case studies. National and regional workshops were co-ordinated. WAY was also represented at the 1994 UN Population conference to obtain the latest information on global population. At the same time, an inter-country workshop was organised in Copenhagen to engage national youth councils.

The Handbook contained the following examples of projects, to assist in the development of new project ideas, including:

- A survey of the sexual behaviour of young people carried out by the World Assembly of Youth in conjunction with the World Organisation of the Scout Movement and the World Health Organisation. This project featured young people themselves developing and carrying out surveys about young people's sexual knowledge, attitudes and behaviours in East, Southern and West Africa;

- Teenage Theatre Speaks to Teens in Canada – young people in Ottawa, Canada were learning about family planning and sexuality through the efforts of a teenage theatre company. Insight theatres, set up by Planned Parenthood Ottawa, toured high schools performing sketches on issues like homosexuality, pregnancy and single motherhood.

- The Society for a New Generation – a youth volunteer group at the Family Planning Association of Hong Kong carried out a varied programme that included family life education in schools and factories, a telephone hotline and clinical services.

- Reaching Young People through Rock: Tatiana and Johnny in Mexico – this project was an effort to promote sexuality, family planning and STD prevention information to young people in Mexico through Rock music. 'Tatiana and Johnny' were a popular rock duo who sang about issues relevant to the young people of Mexico – issues of chastity, faithfulness and the 'macho' pride which makes men reluctant to use contraceptives. The duo's songs were once at the top of the hits charts in Mexico.

Project outcomes

Due to the involvement of young people at all stages of the project, the final document, *The Youth and Population Handbook*, was well received worldwide. Many national youth councils then designed and implemented projects based on the information in the Handbook. The projects that resulted from the Handbook included an Adolescent Fertility Education Programme in the Philippines, AIDS and STD prevention campaigns in Europe, family planning education in Chile, peer to peer AIDS prevention in the USA and peer education on sexuality issues in Jamaica. The verdict – to get the best results for young people, let them do it themselves!

As they were the centre of the consultations, their ideas were the basis of the final document.

One of the main reasons of developing a population handbook was to enable young people to make the right decisions about reproductive health and other population issues. The project therefore empowered both the co-ordinators and the beneficiaries with better information for decision-making.

Case Study 9

Young Ambassadors of Positive Living

Freddie Mubitelela, President and Mathew Miti, Co-ordinator in Zambia

Young Ambassadors of Positive Living (YAPL) is a programme initiated by the Commonwealth Youth Programme (CYP) Africa Centre in response to the spread of HIV/AIDS among young people. It is a youth-run, youth-focused non-profit NGO. Its head office is in Lusaka, Zambia and it has branches countrywide. There are over 50 registered members with Young Ambassadors, all open about their HIV positive status.

The main objective of the programme is to enable young men and women living with the virus to exchange personal experiences with their peers, and to create public awareness by promoting dialogue on the need for increased HIV/AIDS programmes for young people. This dialogue needs to take place among young people living with the virus, their local communities, NGOs and governments.

CYP provides assistance to the Young Ambassadors by offering them administrative, technical and financial support (for example, sponsoring them to attend conferences). CYP also works in partnership with the Ambassadors for HIV/AIDS events, such as the recent Youth Forum in April 2001. However, YAPL is an independent organisation that stands on its own.

The governments of the countries where YAPL operates provide varying degrees of financial and technical support.

YAPL recruits through CYP Africa contact points, and national AIDS control and prevention officers. Ambassadors have good communication skills and proven records of education and outreach efforts in the area of HIV/AIDS. Their main task is to improve the quality of life for young people living with HIV/AIDS through the formation of support groups.

Other objectives include:

- To help young people be self-sufficient economically through the support groups;

- To help reduce the stigma attached to young people with HIV/AIDS through the sharing of personal experiences;

- To promote and protect the rights, interest, participation and responsibility of people living with HIV/AIDS;

- To prevent HIV infections through promoting behaviour change.

Our main activities involve outreach, networking, income-generation and support.

Young Ambassadors visit primary and secondary schools, giving personal experiences of positive living as well as disseminating information about HIV/AIDS through video and drama. Young Ambassadors also give health talks to out-patients, TB patients, and to ante-natal, post-natal and lactating women. We conduct our health talks in a variety of locations, including clinics, work places, local markets and bars. In our effort to facilitate economic self-sufficiency for HIV-positive young people we have conducted tie-and-dye, papier maché and candle-making programmes. We also make home visits to patients and are committed to giving emotional, spiritual and physical support to those who need it.

YAPL is affiliated to the Network of Zambian People Living with HIV/AIDS. We also network with other NGOs, community-based organisations (CBOs), government departments and churches.

The organisation continues to carry out advocacy through high-profile local and information events such as World AIDS Day, candlelight memorials, international conferences on AIDS and STDs in Africa (ICASA) and its own annual general conference. Young Ambassadors are also involved in the government HIV/AIDS television and radio programmes. This helps us to reach young people in remote rural areas.

Our future plans are to advocate for the full participation of young persons in AIDS impact mitigation efforts, at both the grassroots and national levels. We also hope to consolidate the Legal Branch of the network. We will advocate for the establishment of specialised HIV clinics and improvement in access services for health care for all.

When the Young Ambassadors Programme started in Zambia, it had just three young persons. It was difficult for people to join the programme due to the social stigma attached. Now we have more than 30 young people in the programme who have turned out to be role models in our country. These young people, through their bravery, have helped to break the stigma attached to HIV/AIDS.

Mathew Miti: A long road to YAPL

My name is Matthew Miti. I am Zambian and I was born on 29 September 1975, the second in a family of five. I have completed my primary and secondary school education. My mother died in 1994 when I was writing my secondary school final examinations. She was the breadwinner for our family. My father was not working. Therefore I could not continue with further education, as there was no-one to pay for it.

I engaged myself in raising funds so that I could continue school. I started by selling second-hand clothes. Later on I started running a bottle-store and I made a lot of money. A lot of girls came close to me. I got involved with one whom I planned to marry, but later on she died. I did not know what killed her.

In March 1998, I got sick. I was so thin I was weighing 39 kilograms. I went to the hospital where tuberculosis was diagnosed. In our Zambian community once one is said to have TB people conclude by saying that it is AIDS and this happened to me. People were saying that I had AIDS. This made me so sad and the only solution to prove them wrong was for me to undergo an HIV test.

I then went to Kara Counselling to have an HIV test. I was counselled before taking the test. The counsellor probed my previous sexual life. I told him that I had had two girl friends and that I was very intimate with one them. The counsellor asked me if I had received sex education from my parents, teachers, the church or even from friends, and whether I knew anything about STDs. I told him I had never discussed sexual issues with my parents, as it is a taboo in our tradition. The only people I could really discuss matters of sex with were my grandparents. However, they lived far away and we did not communicate. I told him that I had talked about sex with friends. Also our science teacher sometimes mentioned one or two things about sex, but it was only when we were learning reproductive health. After the counselling session, I learned more about HIV/AIDS, its mode of transmission and how it can be prevented.

The counsellor then took the blood sample and asked me to come back for the results the following morning. The following morning I did not go for my results. I was afraid of being found HIV-positive and that I might end up taking my own life, as this would bring shame not only on me but also on my family and my friends. Two weeks later, I convinced myself that it was tuberculosis that I had, and not HIV. So I went for my results. I did not find the counsellor whom I had met the last time. Instead, I found a different man who again counselled me before giving me the results. He first asked me if I was ready for the results and I agreed. He then showed me a paper with 'REACTIVE' in big letters. I did not understand what this meant. He then told me was that I was HIV-positive.

'So instead of proving the people of the community wrong, I am now proven wrong', I said to myself deep down in my heart and I started crying. I saw death two steps ahead of me. The counsellor gave me words of encouragement, 'Mathew! This is not the end of your life but it is the beginning of your new life'. He later referred me to Hope House, a centre for Kara Counselling where people who have been tested HIV-positive are trained on how they can live long with the HIV virus. During this period one can also be trained in some skills such as tailoring, papier maché, candle-making, batik, and tie and dye. I joined the group of people living with HIV/AIDS (PLWHAs) and slowly I started coping with the virus. I was the youngest at the Centre. I did not tell my family that I was going to Hope House. I did not want anyone to know about my status, for fear of being victimised or being discriminated against.

At Hope House I became so active in the field of HIV/AIDS that in no time I was chosen as the chairperson. I was later introduced to the Network of Zambian People Living with HIV/AIDS (NZP+). At NZP+, I was again chosen as the Secretary for Lusaka province, which has more than 200 PLWHAs as its registered members. Lusaka province also has 31 support groups for PLWHAs in various communities. As a chairperson at Hope House and a Secretary for NZP+, I was able to attend a lot of AIDS workshops, and I gained recognition from many HIV/AIDS sister organisations and people.

In December 1998, one of my friends went to a meeting in South Africa and met some people from MTV in America. They wanted a young man in Africa who could do a documentary with them depicting the theme for that year which was AIDS: CHILDREN AND YOUNG PEOPLE. A friend proposed my name without my consent. When he came back, he persuaded me to do the documentary, since it wouldn't be on our local television.

The television crew came and it was time to do the recording. One of the scenes would be recorded at my parents place where I was staying. I ensured that at the time we would be shooting the documentary, my father and my stepmother would not be at home. But when we reached home, I was surprised when I found my father there. My father was also surprised to see me with the 'muzungus' (white people). He asked me about the delegation and I lied to him. I told him that we were recording a drama play and one of the scenes was to be shot at home. My father did not argue when he heard this and he gave us the go ahead.

When we were doing the shooting, it appeared that the Zambian television crew also heard about the delegation and the programme they had come for. They also became interested. They approached me to ask if I could also take part in a short television clip called 'Health Beat'. I tried to refuse by telling them that I did not want to be seen on our local television. But they told me that it was not going to be a long clip and not many people would see or pay much attention to it. I then accepted and they filmed me.

On 1 December 1998 I came home from Hope House as usual and was relaxing in my bedroom. My family was watching TV in the living room, when suddenly I heard my young brother calling me in panic, 'Mathew, Mathew, hurry come and see'. I rushed outside. My brother pointed to the television. It was me. Under the picture were the words written, 'MATHEW MITI – **HIV POSITIVE**'.

I knew that everyone in the world had now watched me. I felt so humiliated, black-mailed, disgusting – I even hated myself. I rushed to the bedroom and the first thing that came into my mind was to commit suicide. I started searching the room for a possible thing that could assist me to reach heaven in time. I then heard someone banging and pushing the door, which I had locked. And within the shortest period the door was opened and Dad entered. I thought to myself, 'Thank God Dad is here'. I expected Dad to help me die by beating me so hard for having being a disgrace to him and the family.

Dad then started by saying, 'I did not know that you could be so brave, my son. You should have told me the time you were shooting the programme. I would have assisted you in one way or the other.'

'I knew about your HIV-positive status before you knew it. Anyway, keep up the good job you have started. But you have to be strong with the community out there. Most *people you think love you will now shun you', Dad said compassionately.*

For almost two weeks, I did not come out of the house for fear of people's reaction. The following week I decided to go to Hope House. I expected to be comforted, congratulated and encouraged by my friends at Hope House. When I reached Hope House I was late. Everybody was in class. When I entered the classroom, everyone looked at me as if I was a stranger. They kept quiet for a moment as if I had died. Then one of them started talking to me. He said, 'Mathew, just how could you disgrace yourself like that on television?' Others followed by saying, 'We have also been disgraced, for every person who sees us here at Hope House will now know that we are all HIV positive.' I was condemned by nearly everybody at Hope House. Instead of being a place of hope for me it became a place of misery.

I then decided to go and seek counselling. The counsellor advised me just like my father did and encouraged me to continue sharing my experience. He then suggested I join the outreach team, which is responsible for disseminating information in schools, churches, colleges, universities, workplaces and the community at large.

Since then, I have ignored people who were saying bad things about me. People started telling my brothers and sisters that they were also suffering from AIDS simply because we were staying in the same house. This made me feel very bad and I moved out. I rented a house in another compound. I had nothing in the house apart from my clothes, one blanket, an electric plate and some plates for cooking. I gave my life to AIDS prevention work. Now, I am well recognised in my country. A lot of young people come to me for counselling, as I am now a trained counsellor. I have helped to break the stigma, though it persists. To help me with my work I joined YAPL. With them I have been to Zimbabwe and Mozambique.

YAPL's achievements ...

- Young people are now starting to accept that AIDS is real and there is some behavioural change among them. Though behaviour change is a long process, we try to revisit them until positive change is attained. Currently the spread of HIV/AIDS in Zambia has stabilised.

- Parent-to-child sexual education has improved. In schools the Zambian government is trying to put sexual education into its curriculum.

- The government, organisations and individuals have started to appreciate the work we are doing. Some organisations, like the Zambia Integrated Health Programme (ZIHP), have included me in their youth advisory committee and their designing team, called the HEART CAMPAIGN. HEART means Helping Each other Act Responsibly Together. This campaign team is also responsible for designing the behaviour change and condom advertisements, and messages on television and radio in seven local languages.

Challenges

- The main difficulty is lack of funding. Since its inception this programme has never been funded. We just use our initiative. Sometimes, the Commonwealth Youth Programme helps us with some logistics, but only when we are invited outside the country.

- Some young people still can't change their behaviour despite having information about AIDS.

- Stigma also prevents young people who are living with HIV/AIDS from getting involved in this programme.

Our hope

We want the government, NGOs and individuals to take up and support this programme.

Our aim is not to transmit HIV/AIDS to others, but to impart good morals and behaviour change.

Case Study 10

Population Control though the Empowerment of Adolescent Girls in Mewat, India

About the organisation

The Society for Promotion of Youth and Masses (SPYM) is an NGO founded in 1983 by Dr Rajesh Kumar. It has 22 regional branches concentrated mostly in the northern and north-eastern states of India. Most of the members and staff of SPYM are young people. The pillars on which SPYM carries out its health and development work are efficiency, trust and sustainability.

SPYM's Motto is 'Be Your Own Light', inspired by the saying of Lord Buddha, 'Self-Help Is The Best Help'.

SPYM's Mission is to provide quality services within the available resources, to enable people to maximise their potential and to increase their abilities, preserve and enhance human dignity and worth, and prevent or reduce the need for service.

SPYM's objectives

- Building the confidence and skills of marginalised communities;
- Promoting gender justice;
- Influencing public and political attitudes towards the recurring problems;
- Addressing the complex links between ignorance and diseases such as HIV/AIDS.

SPYM's reproductive health programmes work to increase community access to appropriate reproductive health care services. They aim to improve the quality of reproductive health services through training and to create demand for those services in the community. SPYM ensures that projects are sensitive to local beliefs and can be sustained in the long term. SPYM's significant contributions in the areas of health and development earned it the prestigious National Youth Award in 1990, presented by the Prime Minister of India.

How the Mewat adolescent project came about

SPYM has been forming and sustaining women's self-help groups (SHGs) in Mewat, northern India, since 1995. Members of the SHGs voiced the need to focus also on adolescents and, based on their request, the project was drawn up. It was conceptualised in consultation with the beneficiaries and other stakeholders.

Area profile

Average age of marriage for boys: 19

Average age of marriage for girls: 13

Average family size: 9.5 members

Mewat is the land of proud and valiant warrior Meos, situated in the southern part of the districts of Gurgaon and Faridabad in Haryana State. The Meos are predominately Muslims, although their beliefs, customs and rituals are a mix of Hinduism and Islam. Located about 120 km south of Delhi, the area is sandwiched between the southern and western Aravalli ranges. In spite of being very near to the capital of the country, the people are not well versed in developmental activities. Many people live below the poverty line and the education level is very low. The condition of the women is very unfortunate. They are politically, socially and economically exploited by their male counterparts. Forms of gender discrimination that are in evidence include wife battering, the dowry system, forced marriages, and deprivation of education, healthcare and nutrition.

Women usually work about 18 hours a day, from 4 am in the morning until 10 pm at night. Most men do not take part in household work. Even in agricultural work, women's share is much greater than men's. Besides this, women collect firewood and provide care for children and other members of their family.

In theory women enjoy 33 per cent representation in the Panchayat Raj institution. However, often it is husbands, father-in-laws and sons who attend on their behalf, as they are considered more knowledgeable and able. Furthermore, suggestions by the few elected women for improving the situation are not taken seriously. Often they are not informed about the agenda or the dates of the meetings. Orthodox traditions, illiteracy and the caste system all inform this lack of political participation by women.

Girls usually do not go to school and form one of the most neglected sections of Mewati society. They lack self-esteem, as they are engaged full-time in household chores and looking after their younger siblings. There are no avenues available to girls to learn and develop skills. Men do not care much about the health problems of the girl child. The girls are physically and psychologically unprepared for childbirth, which they experience around age 15. Accordingly they cannot give proper care and attention to their children. They do not receive medical check-ups, or natal/ante-natal vaccines, and this is a hazard to both mothers and children. The deliveries usually take place at home attended by untrained dias using unsterilised knives and blades, which causes serious health complications and mortalities. By the time women are 20–25 they have already produced four or five children.

SPYM/HIPA's baseline survey in the target area found that STI/RTI prevalence is high. The awareness level regarding reproductive health and contraception, STIs/HIV/AIDS and RTIs and safer sex practices is low. Hygiene is poor. Many women suffer from anaemia, RTIs/STIs, malnutrition, leucorrhoea, premature deliveries and problems related to their menstrual cycle. Men commonly have unprotected sex and use drugs and alcohol, raising the risk of infections within the local population as a whole.

Project goal, objectives and inputs

Goal: Empowerment of 250 adolescent girls of the Mewat area through family life education and skill building over the period of one year, through:

1. Vocational Training

2. Family Life Education (FLE)

3. IEC activity

4. Clinic based services

5. Advocacy and networking.

Objectives:

- To form ten self-help groups of adolescent girls, comprising 25 members each, in five villages;

- To develop vocational skills such as cutting, tailoring and stitching embroidery in two cycles of six months each;

- To impart Family Life Education (FLE) in weekly group sessions;

- To train 20 peer educators to provide information and sustain development;

- To undertake advocacy and network with PHCs and other health agencies for the provision of contraceptives, immunisation and also to route their resources/ services through self help groups.

The following activities were carried out to achieve the goal of the project:

- Creation of self-help groups

  Develop and pre-test the Performa for baseline survey.

  Collect and compile data.

  Procure a list of probable adolescent SHG members. Visit the houses of SHG members. Mobilise and motivate them to join meetings. Start the formation of adolescent SHGs. List the expectations of the girls as well as what their contributions will be.

  Form and train adolescent SHGs through meetings in five villages of the project area.

  Invite resource persons and other SHG members to address SHGs.

List their expectations as well as what their contributions will be.

Hold regular meetings of SHGs.

- Vocational training

The basic thrust of this activity is skill-building and making this an entry point amongst the adolescent women for family life education (FLE).

Identify existing vocational trainer and mobilise resources such as a free place for training, and tools and raw materials for the vocational centre.

Identify trainer for Family Life Education. Conduct FLE training for project staff. Prepare course schedule for adolescent SHG members and conduct one session per week for six months or 48 hours (which ever is earlier) with all the SHG members. This means that the 24-hour module will be implemented in three months and the same will be repeated in the next three months for reinforcement.

- Advocacy and networking

Establish network with line departments for better service delivery.

Visit important line departments on regular basis.

Organise meetings with line departments.

Monitoring, supervision and evaluation plan

A project monitoring committee was formed with a Project Director, Project Co-ordinator and two representatives from the local community. To assess the progress of the programme, the co-ordinator will visit the whole target area on monthly basis. S/he will also talk to beneficiaries and local community leaders and SHG members to ensure the smooth functioning of the project. The project co-ordinator will organise monthly meetings with the educators/trainers to discuss the achievements and plan for further actions and activities. During these meetings all educators trainers will submit their progress reports to the Co-ordinator. The meetings will ensure regular feedback, and that necessary changes are made, with the help of input provided by the local beneficiaries and the field staff.

Sustainability plan

- All the existing adolescent SHGs will be handed over to the main Mewat area development project for further growth.
- All SHG members were encouraged to produce products and sell them in the local market.

- Micro-credit was arranged for the SHGs from the local rural bank.

- Peer educators were encouraged to impart education to other village women on Family Life Education.

Project achievements

Although mothers were willing to send their daughters to Family Life Education sessions, their fathers were reluctant. That 250 girls participated must be counted as a success, and a tribute to the SHG facilitators and to SPYM's credibility. To determine what the young participants felt about the project, we organised Focus Group Discussions (FGDs). The report of one of the FGDs is as follows:

FOCUS GROUP DISCUSSION

The focus group discussion was organised with a sample of 15 participants with whom SPYM had been having regular sessions on Family Life Education. The following was the response from the participants during the FGD in Hathin, Mewat.

What have you learned so far from the sessions? What new things in this programme did you like or feel good about? Was there anything that you didn't like?

- With the passage of time we should change ourselves and our thinking.

- We have learned skills like stitching, cutting and tailoring.

- The vocational skills will make us self-sufficient as we can earn.

- The programme has certainly helped us to understand where we stand.

- Day by day we have learned something new from this programme.

- By sharing each other's experiences we can learn the prevailing pros and cons of our society.

- We are also now aware of some games.

- We have certainly developed a vision to plan our future.

- We are getting time and opportunity to discuss many things that we cannot discuss with our parents.

- We can think about changing traditions.

- We have a platform to think and share differently.

- It is bad to comment on others.

- Each and every individual is unique in themselves, in matters of choices, preferences and behaviour, so one must not be judgmental.

- It is not only girls but boys too who suffer.

- There should be equal division of labour at home and also in other fields.
- There is nothing we did not like.

Has your level of knowledge and awareness of the issues dealt with increased?

- Yes, we have become more punctual.
- We have learned the importance of feelings and emotions and any doubt on something without confirmation can be harmful in any relationship.
- We share each and everything frankly that we think and feel.
- We could discuss what we have learned and explore it.
- We could learn about ourselves ('ZABAN AA GAI').

How do you feel, and what you have learned, now the programme is over?

- We are feeling very sad and uncomfortable as we are separated from each other after having a good time.
- In future we are not sure that we will get any chance to participate in such a programme.
- We have benefited a lot from this programme.
- Our thinking has developed and now we can plan for our better future.
- We have developed communication and listening skills.
- We are much more aware about sex.
- We learned about health issues.
- Now we are comfortable and mature enough to discuss topics like puberty.
- We now understand the advantages of having a small family.
- Now we have specific goals in our lives and for that we are putting our maximum efforts.
- We are now able to plan our career.
- Now we can express our feelings quite confidently in front of others.
- Before when we did something we used never to think of consequences, but now we are very much concerned about consequences.
- Now we have realised that instead of changing society we must change ourselves as each one of us is part of it. By changing ourselves we can change the whole society.
- We would love to have such programmes for all the youth of this country.

Would you now reach out to the other girls in their community, who have not gone through this programme? How would you do this?

All the participants said they would help in:

- Involving more girls in their villages in such programmes;
- Making space available and doing other things that were a prerequisite of organising the programme.

Conclusions

Trends, patterns and lessons

Youth-led and *youth-driven* movements can be viable and earn credibility purely on the strength of their actions and message. As for those organisations created by *adults* for youth advancement, the most effective ones have succeeded in building skills and confidence in their youth, to a point that they are able to participate in their own right in the life of the organisation. In other words, they have enlisted youth as partners, rather than as 'objects' or 'targets' of their programmes.

These institutional studies illustrate young people's ability and desire to organise around topics of interest, to forge links to achieve objectives, and to sustain the enriching and educative experiences of their lives. We have chosen a few discussion themes out of the dozens of possibilities presented by the case studies.

Think differently

- Drik's Out of Focus project is unusual – it uses a visual medium, photography, to enable self-expression in working class youth.

- The EDGE case study reveals creative use of multi-media and advanced technology by young people to disseminate their messages. Bluepeace campaigners brought their issue into the mainstream by distributing T-shirts and stickers to the public. They also published an easy-to-use reference book on an eco-friendly lifestyle which generated so much interest that it is now part of the primary school curriculum in the Maldives.

- The informal and creative format of the SPYM's self-help groups seems to have been enabling and fun for the young girls, encouraging them to think of reproductive health options they previously did not have access to.

- *collective echoes* emphasised creative use of the public space and used locally available materials to articulate young people's artistic aspirations.

- WAY's Youth and Population Handbook project documents successful and creative approaches to educating youth on reproductive health issues. The Handbook itself is an innovation, as it draws young people into a dialogue on a daunting topic.

Youth movements and schemes have captured the public imagination when they have promoted unconventional thinking. The best youth movements have offered new paradigms, new ways of thinking, knowing and being.

Multi-generational learning

It is well-known that young people learn best from their peers. Often young people can be understood only by their peers. The Connect Youth visit to Malawi provides a good illustration. AYISE, a youth centre based in Blantyre, assisted a local hospital in its efforts to provide good health care for young people by engaging with young people's language. As suggested by the Self Help Groups of SPYM, the co-mentorship model of *collective echoes*, the photography training by Drik and the HIV/AIDS counselling sessions in the YAPL study, *once trust is established*, young people will learn from adults just as well as they do from their peers. The most successful youth initiatives have been holistic in their approach, involving sympathetic elders and the wisdom of multiple generations, and ultimately earning respect for youth within their communities and beyond.

Effective use of technology, print and electronic media

Many of the organisations featured here have taken advantage of the technological revolution to reach a wider audience and to widen their network of partners. Drik is a pioneer in the information and communications technology field in Bangladesh. EDGE uses multimedia, including movies shot by youth members, to encourage interest in eco-tourism and sustainable development. YAPL activists regularly target the media to engage youth in discussions on HIV/AIDS.

Nonetheless, we must recognise that the 'digital divide' is more than a cliché. It is a reality in many societies around the world. Indeed, several youth organisations are increasingly mindful of the fact that, in some parts of the world, children do not have access to basic literacy or to a black board and chalk, let alone to computers. Since English is the major language of the internet, there is also a concern that non-English speakers may be left out of interesting youth initiatives.

Information and knowledge

Ours is the information age, and the era of information technology. As vital as 'information' is, it is not an end in itself. Many of the case studies prove that information has to be mediated locally if it is to have an effect. SPYM encourages young girls to think about reproductive health in the context of their own lives in traditional patriarchal communities.

All roads lead to the community

One of the most important themes that emerges from these institutional studies is that of the mutual empowerment of youth and their communities. As illustrated by the Pachen Village case study, 'young people readily take on responsibility if they have a sense of ownership'. If young people are engaged as full partners in the life and development of the community, the ultimate winner is the community itself. As illustrated by the Drik and *collective echoes* experiences, the community might even take a while to understand or welcome the new initiatives. The experiences of the youth of BluePeace, Pachen Village, YAPL and other organisations also attest to their ability to reach out from communities to government agencies, politicians, foreign donors and others. In NGO parlance, this is known as 'multistakeholder involvement'. Over and over again, the lesson we draw is that there can be no 'community' without youth.

Think locally and globally – act locally and globally

Young people must be consciously and systematically involved in seeking solutions to 'global' problems, even when they are traditionally 'adult' issues. No issue is out of reach, because adult decisions affect every aspect of our lives every day. IPPF and WAY are both international youth organisations dealing with 'serious' adult issues such as planned parenthood and global population. YAPL and SPYM operate at the national and regional levels, dealing respectively with HIV/AIDS and reproductive health.

EDGE and Connect Youth are both national youth initiatives, with a consciously international outlook. EDGE members, like Bluepeace members, attend international conferences on the environment and sustainable development. Connect Youth conducts international study trips for youth who might not normally have the chance to go abroad and learn about the world. Ultimately, all the youth initiatives described here have an impact on global discussions.

Common goals but different starting points

Drik was created to 'right a wrong'. In the words of Drik's founder, Shahidul Alam, 'Western media had created an image that was distorted….' Their country, Bangladesh, was known for all the wrong reasons. This is illustrative of the divisions characterising our 'global village', both across and within social units of every scale. Although we talk about common global problems, ours is a fractured human community. Many of the youth organisations represented here have to take this into account. *collective echoes* insisted on diversity training for its members, to reflect Vancouver's ethnic mix. WAY and IPPF have been diligent in putting together truly international and representative youth committees, so they can meaningfully discuss global topics such as population and planned parenthood. A large element of YAPL's effort is concerned with the stigma attached to this already cruel disease, and to reintegrate those with HIV/AIDS into the mainstream of society.

Creating enabling structures for youth participation

Youth perspectives are sometimes different from prevailing norms, and youth empowerment might entail replacing debilitating structures and installing norms and systems that better reflect young people's needs and abilities. The IPPF case study describes the process of institutionalising youth participation within an organisation. Youth participants of the Working Group concluded that young people must be valued for their individual contributions. But achieving this may require structural transformation. *collective echoes* deliberately adopted a daring and inclusive approach in its organisational structure which, although perceived as 'different' by donors, accurately reflected Vancouver's multi-ethnicity and multi-culturalism.

Multiplier-effect or ripple effect

Effective programmes have, almost without fail, generated other follow-up or wholly new initiatives. SPYM had been organising women's self-help groups for many years. The SHG for adolescent girls featured in this chapter was created at the request of the women who had benefited from these SHGs. EDGE provides the most dramatic illustration of one successful youth initiative engendering another. The WAY *Youth and Population Handbook* has led to many creative youth initiatives around the world. Bluepeace activists talk about the 'multiplier' effect within their movement, as their message caught on among the public, and other NGOs in Maldives started taking up the cause of saving turtles and conserving the environment.

Keeping the focus: sustaining youth participation

The success of the Bluepeace initiative lies in its remarkable ability to learn from mistakes, consistently come up with alternative solutions and never lose sight of its campaign goals. When Bluepeace found that the turtle hatchery project that they had been promoting was actually harmful to the turtles, they quickly conducted further research and came up with alternatives. Idealism and pragmatism also come together in the self-assessment of the members of *collective echoes*; 'large doses of reality need to be part of the equation if this kind of model is to be replicated. Ideally, we wouldn't have forged ahead without secured wage funding ... But our passion and our desire to fulfill the original vision kept us focused on our early goals.'

As we have seen in several instances, focus and passion must be supplemented with real training and skill-building in order to ensuring sustainability of the programmes. For example, SPYM's empowering Family Life Education for young girls was supplemented by vocational training (in tailoring, craft-making etc.). Drik's Out of Focus project crucially imparts marketable skills to the children involved.

Young people need an opportunity, not charity

Not all projects that empower young people are actually initiated by them. Often, an individual or a civil society organisation with the right motivation can reach out and provide the critical first opportunity. To quote from the experience of the Husena Youth Group of Papua New Guinea, 'the "hand-out" mentality as seen in some welfare state or youth grants will only make youth a liability to the nation's development. Good programmes will encourage youth to find their place as productive members of communities.' Drik and SPYM have reached out to young people with a message and an opportunity for skill-building. IPPF and WAY provide opportunities at the international level.

The gift of life and the power of one

While each case study featured here emphasises this final and most important theme, its best illustration is provided by the Young Ambassadors of Positive

Living, who have battled a disease and the attendant social stigma, to bring hope, inspiration and awareness to young people. Each personal pathway to participation, and each individual success story empowers us all. Who can remain unmoved by the statements of Mathew Miti of YAPL and Dana Thorpe of *collective echoes*?

Challenges and future visions

Young people, as we have seen in the statistics quoted in the Chapter 1, and in the analysis of Chapter 2, are the single largest untapped constituency of human potential. Yet social and political organisations across the spectrum are soliciting and using young people to advance their objectives. We have civil society organisations with their message of youth participation for development and peace. On the other hand, young people are invited to participate in their national life by joining the military. We have political parties who mobilise youth as foot soldiers, distributing pamphlets, putting up posters and canvassing in elections, but not as decision-makers.

At the extreme, we have religious, political and civil society organisations with openly xenophobic or racist missions. These organisations, too, actively solicit youth participation. They systematically target young people and recruit them with visions of a better future and purer, stronger communities. The main instrument of inclusion in these cases is explicit exclusion of certain other groups.

Advanced technology means that young people are assaulted everyday by competing ideologies and confusing messages. 'To participate or not' is only part of the problem. Young people also have to confront the issues of how, where and when to participate. They are required to sort through multiple recruiting opportunities, relying only on their best judgments and, if they are lucky, on the advice of family and friends.

Our belief is that robust, versatile and sustainable youth participation – at the level of the individual and the age group as a whole – has to be based on an inclusive approach. This much is obvious. But the dependency is mutual: organisations that wish to promote inclusive societies in the widest sense, must pursue youth participation. They should be aware that their competitors are recruiting the young.

Our vision is one of empowering environments for all young people and their communities, all over the world. We hope these institutional examples show that this is possible.

Chapter 4

Pathways to Personal Empowerment

Charlotte Barran

Contributors to this chapter are from different generations, different continents and very different backgrounds. The one thing they have in common is that they are all active participants in civil society. And more than that, they all began to participate in civil society as young people. In spite of their varied backgrounds, there are common factors that led all of them to participate. There is no magic formula for youth activism, but as this chapter demonstrates, there are magic ingredients.

Youth participation does not require a certain level of education, or a certain level of wealth or status. The nature of youth participation means that it can happen in any economic, political or social environment. Youth participation does not rely on money or democracy. The key components of youth participation are more fundamental than that: a basic recognition of the need to participate in society; positive relationships with adults and peers; and a supportive and enabling physical environment.

In attempting to understand the critical factors which ensure effective and genuine youth participation, we draw on the life experiences of eight individuals from around the world. We have arranged these profiles in chronological order, starting with an activist in her eighties and ending with a teenager. These stories are inspirational and instructive.

80+: **Paula Pelaez Gomez**, Chile

Paula Pelaez Gomez is an Educationalist based in Chile. She has been an active member of the Asociación de Guías y Scouts de Chile throughout her life. Paula has written several books and publications on adolescents.

I am 89 years old and I work in two Youth Centres.

Even though my childhood was a happy one, my teenage years were sad. I was only 14 when my mother died unexpectedly. As I was finishing my secondary education, I once again met with the unexpected – a friend and schoolmate of mine committed suicide.

I wanted to study medicine, but my father, who until then had been 'my love' was stubbornly opposed since at the time (1930) girls who attempted this had to be 'rather mad'. Some felt it was immoral for girls to be face to face with naked dead bodies in front of male colleagues.

I studied civil engineering for a year at the Universidad de Chile until I managed to convince my father to accept my enrolment in the School of Medicine. He imposed conditions on me whereby he did not allow me to go to parties. But I was happy in medicine.

My vital youthful energy was probably strengthened by the love which my parents gave to six children in difficult times. They taught us to face up to difficulties from an early age. We had to be brave and firm. After suffering a setback we had to give thanks that we had overcome it, that we had weathered the storm. Personally, I had in my favour my faith which made me follow Father Alberto Hurtado, for whose 'poor people' I worked ever since the time when I was studying medicine. I learned about the solidarity of those who have little, but who help their fellow men.

Over the years I have seen teenagers moved by the certainty that there is someone out there to whom they matter.

40+: **Catherine Bertini,** Executive Director, United Nations World Food Programme, USA

Catherine Bertini is the Executive Director of the World Food Programme (WFP), the largest global food aid agency. In 1992 she became the first American woman to head a UN organisation and the first woman to lead WFP. In March 2000, she was named the Secretary-General's special envoy to the Horn of Africa. As a teenager, Catherine Bertini had a favourite quotation by Edmund Burke. 'The only thing required for the triumph of evil is for good men and women to do nothing.' Ms Bertini's experiences as a young woman, which included volunteering at a shelter for homeless women, helped her to steer WFP into new policy areas. Ms Bertini believes that women are the key to resolving hunger and that the international community must work to strengthen their ability to cope effectively in crises.

My first interest in public policy was generated by my father's civic involvement. He ran for city councillor when I was 13, and I organised other young teenagers to distribute his campaign literature. After he was elected I went to city council meetings to watch him work, and from then on I was interested in government.

Suggestions from adults made a difference as well. Women Air Force Officers based in South Vietnam told me of citizens' needs there and I organised a campaign to raise resources for them. My father's political party ran a week-long seminar for high school students. Finally, my social studies and geography teachers were brilliant.

All this had an impact, and then there was the Girl Scouts. I recall proudly serving as Mayor for a Day through the Girl Scouts programme!

Girl Scouting had a big influence on me as a young woman. My leaders encouraged me to set goals and work to achieve them.

As a young woman I remember reading a biography of Elizabeth Blackwell, the first American woman to become a medical doctor. Her story inspired me to follow my own dream. I believe that young girls and women should dare to follow their dream, whatever it may be, and let no obstacles stand in their way.

30s: Alphonsine Kabagabo, Regional Executive for Africa, World Association of Girl Guides and Girl Scouts (WAGGGS)

In 1994 Alphonsine fled Rwanda with her 6-month-old daughter because of the civil war. Alphonsine has been WAGGGS Regional Executive for Africa since March 1998. She is responsible for helping the region to implement quality Guiding programmes to meet the needs of young women in Africa. The World Association of Girl Guides and Girl Scouts consists of five regions, with 140 member organisations and 10 million individual members.

I have been active in youth movements since the age of 12 when I began to take on responsibilities in the Guide Association based at my school.

I wanted to join a youth organisation because I wanted to do something within my community to contribute towards the improvement of people's lives, to make a change, and also because I was convinced that by pooling our strengths the impact would be greater.

My role model is without doubt my father. Ever since I was very young I saw that he took an interest in social issues and I saw him get involved in community activities. He always encouraged me to join youth movements so that I might be exposed to the outside world and play a role in the community, and therefore gain skills other than academic ones.

I was 16 years old when I became active. I was in charge of the Guide Association at my school and I also represented the school in national youth organisations and at the Ministry of Youth and Ministry of Education. This gave me the opportunity to take part in organising many meetings and demonstrations where the grievances of young people were expressed.

At the age of 22, I became one of the National Leaders of the Guides of Rwanda and I was responsible for public and international relations. I was also a member of the National Council for Youth.

I am convinced that this active participation has really broadened my mind, has given me a sense of responsibility, of teamwork, of respect for my fellow human beings and has empowered me for life.

Active participation in youth movements has allowed me and other young women to deal with the ethnic divisions which are tearing Rwandan society apart, and to take more of an interest in the development of society in general.

However, our participation in Rwanda's civil society was limited by the fact that politicians wanted to use us to achieve their goal, which limited what we did and the impact of it.

I am currently the Executive for the Africa Region at WAGGGS. In this role I work with thousands of young women in Africa and I am absolutely convinced that their participation allows them to grow up with confidence, an open mind, and a desire to contribute to positive changes within society. They grow into more responsible adults who will make a difference, however small that might be.

Finally, I am sure that my active participation in youth movements has given me skills and the ability to carry out the work I do today, perhaps even more than my studies at university.

Africa is a continent where the majority of the population is young. However, participation in youth movements is very limited. If only there were more young people who had the opportunity to become active and to obtain skills which would allow them to become good citizens, there would be more positive changes, perhaps even less violence and less hatred.

Ashok Pillai, President, Indian Network for People living with HIV

The Indian Network for People living with HIV/AIDS (INP+) aims to give a voice to people living with HIV/AIDS, especially women and children, and to counter the fear, ignorance and prejudice surrounding the problem.

I am Ashok Pillai, a young man 32 years old. I come from a village in Uttar Pradesh. In 1987, at the age of 19, I joined the Indian Navy ready to take on the world. Things took a new turn when I tested positive for HIV in 1989.

In 1992 I left the Navy as I had contracted tuberculosis. I went back to my home town. I was living life the way I wanted, because according to my doctors I had only three or four years to live. So I spent all my savings and withstood the pressure from my father to complete my graduation. Lacking any information on HIV or positive living, I was in the prime of my life, left with nothing to do, living life by the day.

I realised that my family – four sisters and my elderly parents – would be hurt if I died suddenly without telling them about me. Eventually, when they wanted me to get married, I told my father about my HIV status and slowly I told the rest of my family. They took it in their stride. They supported me morally, and they never once asked how I got HIV. Their belief in me, and their support, has given me the strength to go on.

My life's most remarkable experience came in 1996 in the form an invitation to a meeting in Pune, which was for people living with HIV. There I met young people who, like me, were HIV-positive, but were facing discrimination from family, friends and society. There was an urge among the participants of the meeting to form a network of people living with HIV, our own network to raise our issues.

I volunteered to do everything that would make this dream a reality. In 1997, together with 11 others, I formed INP+. I finally found a purpose in my life. From the need felt by people living with HIV there grew a movement for change. We now have around a thousand members all over India; most of us are in the 30–35 age group.

As the President of a national network of people living with HIV, I am an activist, an advocate, a speaker, a strategist, a negotiator, an administrator, a trainer and more. Above all, I am a treatment activist; the main focus for me is access to treatment for people living with HIV. I know by personal experience that young people with HIV die because they are born in this country and have no way to access treatment. I have seen how the antiretroviral drugs have changed the life of people in a positive way and I want that for my fellow people. I am also worried about the vulnerability of young people to HIV, as I became positive at a very young age.

I am very open about my status. An HIV-positive speaker can build confidence in people who have not yet come out due to fear of discrimination. Telling a person who has tested positive that I have been living with HIV for 12 years makes a difference to how they look at their future. Together with other members, I have tried to be the voice of millions living with HIV.

Living with HIV and being young has provided me with challenges and dreams that I never dared confront before. Life itself has been the best classroom. I have developed strategies to address the issues of people living with HIV and I have improvised and fine-tuned my skills as I went along.

Young people are very easy to work with. If they are entrusted with responsibility they are less likely to let you down. Young people should be involved in planning and follow through to decision-making. INP+ is a movement of young people and is the response of young people living with HIV to this epidemic. I always tell my fellow people living with HIV that participation is when you give yourself completely in to what you do, so that you become one with it and I think that it holds good for youth participation too.

20s: **Henry Zakumumpa, Head of the Radio Division, Straight Talk, Uganda**

Straight Talk is a local Ugandan Health Communications NGO targeting adolescents as part of the prevention of HIV/AIDS among young people. It spreads adolescent sexual and reproductive health messages through the radio, newspapers and its Outreach to Schools Programme.

My activism as a youth, as far as I remember, began early on in school. At 15, I became the Chairman of the Junior Debating Club at Mbarara High School. I vividly remember leading my dormitory to winning the 1992 inter-house debating competitions and sweeping the coveted prize, the Oxford English Dictionary. I had chanced upon the autobiographies of Nelson Mandela and John F. Kennedy in the school library and felt inspired to lead a distinguished life.

At high school, I elected to pursue liberal arts education and moved to Makerere College School in Kampala, where my former school was regarded as 'nondescript'. I strove to excel academically to prove myself and to win the attention of the girls! I was particularly 'loud' in the history class and was always a persistent contributor in inter-school seminars.

By the age of 18, I had come to form part of a circle of like-minded friends from several schools who belonged to the Pan-African Youth Movement, a vibrant youth organisation emphasising pride in traditional heritage.

I was deputy editor of the 'Macorean' – a school magazine and leading student mouth piece against student government excesses. By 1995, I belonged to a network of idealistic, progressive minded young people.

Makerere College School was a very diverse community and in order to preserve our activism we formed the Nakawa Students Association, of which I was elected Secretary-General. We were a community volunteer group penetrating local communities with our message of 'household savings mobilisation'. We initiated contact with civic bodies and with our area MP who was also a Local Government Minister.

Negotiating for a greater student role in the community was a key interest which we campaigned for. I remember that several of my peers and I served as Presiding Officers in the 1996 Uganda presidential polls. Others chose partisan politics and went on to get elected to the statutory youth councils.

In June 1998 many of us completed university, feeling prepared to launch ourselves into the blue yonder world. I remember sitting in the cafeteria with four other friends after our last exam paper and deciding on the next course after school. Development work was the most obvious choice for most of us. I took a particular interest in HIV/AIDS because I considered it to be our country's gravest challenge. At the end of 1998 I joined the Straight Talk Foundation.

At Straight Talk, I have been given an enabling environment and have been welcomed by people with a firm belief in what young people have to offer. In October 1999 I was the youngest organisation representative to sit on a Ugandan Government 'National Anti-AIDS Strategic Policy Framework' Committee. I have had to work hard (perhaps twice as hard as more senior colleagues) to prove worthy of the trust I have been given as a young person.

Although young people have been given the huge responsibility of running Straight Talk, there is still 'inaccessible' territory. No young person sits on the Foundation Board, which is the highest policy making part of the organisation. This makes the young people feel like their participation is 'sphered'.

There has to be a start though ... I am in full control of the radio station – I write the scripts, develop the concepts, manage older staff, conduct interviews, manage the budget, and design the half hour programmes, as well as help in monitoring and evaluation. I am an equal participant in the weekly Monday policy making meetings.

I am 25 now. Next year I plan to go to Graduate School. I hope to move on and allow space for other young blood. ...

Mulako Mwanamwalye, Pan-Commonwealth Youth Caucus Chairperson

The Pan-Commonwealth Youth Caucus is a network of youth leaders who serve as a voice for young people across the 54 member countries of the Commonwealth. It is a consultative mechanism of the Commonwealth Youth Programme.

My name is Mulako Mwanamwalye, a Zambian national born in 1973. I am currently serving as the Pan-Commonwealth Youth Caucus Chairperson (2000–2003) and working full time for the National Youth Council of Zambia as Research and Development Co-ordinator.

Growing up as a girl child in Africa really was the beginning of the struggle to achieve meaningful participation. I have grown up in an environment where a young person should only be seen, not heard, and where adults decide what roles young people should take. In my culture, a young person is not expected to stand in front of adults to speak, except at their request.

It was not until my days at university in the early 1990s, when I joined an association for students of political and administrative studies, that I began to actively participate in youth activities. During that time, my country was undergoing a political transition from a one party state to multi-party democracy. The socio-economic situation was deteriorating at a fast rate and the general population was seeking change. As students we played a significant role in agitating for change and facilitating a smooth transition to a new government. It was then that it occurred to me that young people can and should play an important role in a nation's development process. But now, when I look back, I see how young people are often used to bring about positive change and then dumped.

Working as a Research and Development Co-ordinator for a National Youth Council and serving as a Pan-Commonwealth Youth Caucus Chairperson has given me opportunities to mingle with young people from different ethnic backgrounds, cultures and religions. I have had opportunities to organise a variety of youth fora at national, regional and international levels and see how young people from civil society work with governments, donors, international NGOs and inter-governmental organisations. More importantly, I have also seen how young people interact among themselves.

In all this, I have come to realise that young people all over the world face the same challenge – not being accepted as equal partners in the development process. I have experienced lack of acceptance in my various positions as a young person from both fellow young people who questioned my legitimacy to lead them and the adults who believe that young people do not have the necessary experience.

Having served as Regional Youth Co-ordinator for the Commonwealth Africa Region, I have come to realise that effective youth participation is possible only when the relevant structures are put in place and the required resources are made available. The transfer of skills to young people in all areas that affect their lives is critical in order to bridge the generation gap. These are the lessons to be learned by organisations committed to ensure real participation for young people.

Personally, participation has empowered me to be able to take decisions on my own behalf, and not at the direction of others, in all areas of my life.

My message to the young people out there is that youth participation is not about the next person but about you. Do not allow yourself to be manipulated. Many of us fall prey to tokenism where young people are represented as being involved but have no decision-making power. True participation occurs when young people are involved in all stages of programme development. Don't accept the digital divide. Sharpen your IT skills because access to information is a key ingredient to participation.

Despite the number of barriers that inhibit youth participation, I am very optimistic about the future. I will continue being involved and active in the youth movement.

Edward Registe, Regional Co-ordinator, Commonwealth Youth Caucus

I am 29-year-old Edward Registe. I have been involved in youth work from a very early age. Having been raised in the Catholic faith, I was given many opportunities to interact with my peers from when I was 9-years-old at Sunday School. Sunday School and summer school programmes run by the Youth Development Division in Dominica enabled me to go on several field trips, where I met many new people and made many friends around the island at a very early age.

By the time I was 10, I had secured a government scholarship, which gave me access to secondary education. Since I lived in a rural community where there was no secondary school, I had to commute nine miles daily to school. In those days very few people were given that opportunity and so those of us who got the chance to obtain a secondary education were automatically looked upon as leaders among our peers in our communities. By the age of 16 I was elected president of my church youth organisation and my social youth club.

At school I was an average student and never took up leadership in student activities except my participation in many arguments about issues in the school concerning students.

On leaving formal education, I was part of a team of old school boys who were brought together by the Youth Development Division to look into the feasibility of forming a National Youth Council for Dominica. I was elected to head the steering committee mandated to carry out the feasibility study. It entailed a lot of personal sacrifice and struggle to create a voice for youth in a country that saw its youth as a liability except at election time when they became useful pawns in the political game.

The committee persevered for more than two years until 1996 when we finally established a National Youth Council with strong government backing. I was once again called upon to rise to the challenge of leadership when I was elected as the first President of the Council, a post I held for four years. During that time I and my colleagues learned a lot about youth rights and responsibilities. We were able to motivate Dominican youth to take positive action and we found some success in changing society's negative image of its youth.

Today I still serve as Vice-President of the Caribbean Federation of Youth and I am also the Regional Co-ordinator of the Commonwealth Youth Programme Regional Youth Forum. I am still very involved in other youth organisations.

Youth work has had a very great impact on my life. I have gained many friends and felt very proud that I was able to make a significant contribution towards national and regional development at a very early age, something that many of my young Caribbean contemporaries do not get to do. It has earned me a tremendous amount of respect in my country and I am actually listened to and consulted on many issues. It has been an uphill struggle to change perceptions of young people, enabling them to become important stakeholders in the developmental thrust in my country but I have never regretted a moment of it.

I hope that more resources will be allocated by the governments of the world and international institutions towards youth development programmes. I truly believe that the youth of the world are its most valuable resource and that efforts must be urgently made to genuinely embrace youth participation at all levels in the global community. Only when we have accomplished this will our young people be better motivated to desire a secure and productive future.

Kuh Abigail Pasion, Girl Scouts, Philippines

Kuh Abigail is a Cadet Girl Scout with the Girl Scouts of the Philippines, which is the largest organisation for girls and young women in the Philippines with over a million members. Kuh is in her third year of college at the University of the Philippines.

I was brought up to be responsible for my actions. As long as I can remember, I have been involved in activities that I believed in. My father used to joke about it as youthful exuberance, but he and my family have always been supportive of my actions. My siblings and I grew up in an atmosphere that demanded responsible participation and a genuine desire for truth and change. Of course when you are just about knee high and eating lollipops while trying to point out to your elders what you think is right, you can't expect people to treat you seriously. But this never deterred me, it only made me more persistent.

Even when I was young I have always refrained from being an innocent bystander if I could do something to address an issue. In high school my participation grew as I took on socio-civic responsibilities. I became an officer of our student body organisation, elected to the supreme student council and the editor of our newspaper. I was involved in activities that extended beyond school. I attended the first National Youth Summit where thousands of young people joined forces to address issues affecting youth. I also experienced being part of the local government when I took office as the Junior Mayor of Laoag City. During the time that I was Junior Mayor, we worked with young people involved in drugs and street fighting through our programme, Dance against Drugs. I know that what we did barely scratched the surface, but it was a beginning.

Just before I left for college, I attempted to further my participation in society. I took part in a project against dengue fever as part of the Chief Girl Scout Medal Scheme.

I have to admit that even though I had participated in decision-making, social issues and school activities, my definition of participation had always been a conventional one. In 1999, at the World CIVICUS Assembly, I became more aware of what is happening and I saw how narrow my understanding of rights and participation had been. I had always taken it for granted that the opportunities we enjoy are universally accepted. The stories of discrimination, of women removed from the political and social spectrum because of gender, of young people whose idealism is quashed by tradition, made me realise how greatly we are still deprived of the most basic thing – the right to be heard.

I learned a lot at the CIVICUS conference. And importantly, I began to act on that lesson. When you face the crisis of political instability, when those who should be the protectors of our sovereignty threaten to take it away, when the very institution that should ensure social justice and truth breaks down, young people are left with a great responsibility to take a stand. If participation and empowerment means doing what your conscience and your ideals dictate, and never wavering in your quest for freedom from all kinds of oppression, then indeed I can proudly say that I've experienced it.

But that is not to say that participation is all smooth sailing. We are often hindered by obstacles like being put down because of our age or our limited resources. In the case of the recent uprisings in the Philippines, I endured along with many others the criticism of our families, our peers and the media.

I know that I still have a lot to learn and experience. But I never hesitate to contribute what I can when it is needed. I am currently involved in several student bodies as a volunteer.

Perhaps when the time comes that I can finally say that I really did something is when I see other young people participating. Only then can I finally say that my own participation has made a difference.

10–15-year-olds: **Renata Andrade Garcia,** Girl Guide, Brazil

The Federação de Bandeirantes do Brasil was founded in 1919 and acts today as one of the most important Brazilian institutions working on non-formal education, ensuring active citizenship for children and young people. Renata Andrade is a Girl Guide, belonging to the São Bernardo do Campo in the Sño Paulo District.

What can I say? It was worth it.

I don't really know how it happened. I got into Girl Scouting without even knowing exactly what it was about, what they did or what made people do it! Maybe I was after new challenges and as the saying goes: when you don't know where you want to go, any place will do.

My attitude to life was that I didn't really care and I certainly didn't work very hard.

But then, there was a day ... it was time to rotate the team posts and it was my turn to co-ordinate the team. Me, the ever irresponsible me!

And it was then, at age 13, that I woke up. I didn't have a special someone to look up to. I just set my goals and went after them. I didn't know if I would get there, but I kept going.

I like decision-making. Now I am 13 and I still have a long way to go, I'm thinking of new objectives. I have learned that people don't have the time to think any more, the value of true friendship.

To send young people a message? 'Follow your dreams! Reach for your goals without looking backwards, that means what it is, back, past. Think of the future. Don't let things stop you. Think of the joy of having reached there. And most of all, BE HAPPY.

Critical factors

What are the critical factors which ensure effective and genuine youth participation?

- **A personal commitment**

No-one can force a young person to participate in any real sense. Anyone who recalls his or her schooldays will also recall that the pupil who was made to do something did it reluctantly and half-heartedly. Youth participation can be encouraged but it is ultimately up to the young person themselves to embrace activism.

Ashok spent four years living life exactly how he wanted, ignoring his father's pleas for him to graduate. Instead he lived recklessly, spending all his money. Ashok had to come to the decision himself to invest his time and energy in improving the quality of people living with HIV/AIDS. Ashok chose to participate, and as soon as he did, he finally found the purpose of his life.

All of the authors of the personal pathways made the conscious and voluntary decision to participate.

- **The influence of adults**

Young people may make the decision to participate themselves, but this decision is not reached without key outside influences.

The relationship that young people have with adults can positively or negatively influence the decisions that young people make. Influential adults may be teachers, parents, or community leaders who take on a mentoring role. Adults may influence from a distance – famous figures may provide inspiration.

A parent, often a father, plays a key role in a young person's development. Catherine Bertini organised other young people to participate in her father's political campaign. Equally, a young person can have a profound effect on his or her parents. A young person can challenge the beliefs and values which adults themselves may have established in their youth. A young person can help an adult to recognise that society changes, as do the issues affecting that society. Paula's father had the courage to counter his own wishes for his daughter and allow her to follow her own path – albeit with some provisos.

- **The influence of peers**

Sometimes, adults may seem to be too remote or out of touch, or they may not always be available as more and more young people move away from home to study or to work. Peers play an increasingly crucial role in determining a young person's value system.

Young people are unlikely to be active participants in isolation. Young people need the support and the friendship of peers who are like-minded and who are driven by the same goals. It was when they met as a group that Ashok and other young people living with HIV felt inspired to form a network. Henry met like-minded young people through the Pan-African Youth Movement who became friends and who also influenced each other's career choices. Youth activism enables young people to make friends and strengthen their networks. Edward has gained many friends through his youth work.

All the contributors to this chapter talk about friends who have shared in their activities and their goals.

- **A space to belong**

Even if young people enjoy friendship with like-minded people or with inspiring adults, they cannot become active participants in civil society without a space or an arena in which to develop. A key feature of personal empowerment, as shown in this chapter, is the power of a youth organisation to give confidence and security, and to provide for the development of skills that are not necessarily practised in the home or at school.

Renata and Kuh belong to the Girl Guides or the Girl Scouts. Edward belongs to several youth organisations which have enabled him to develop his own skills as well as lobby on behalf of a significant group. Organised youth activism gives young people a powerful voice with which to lobby governments and impact upon civil society; the National Youth Council of Dominica made a significant impact on the lives of young people in the country. All the personal accounts talk of joining an organisation or a movement in order to achieve personal goals.

Religion also plays a role in providing a space for the development of young people. Both Paula and Edward were involved in church activities. His involvement in Sunday School introduced Edward to peer group learning at a young age. Paula's Catholic faith encouraged her to participate in civil society.

- **A need for change**

It might be AIDS, or poverty, or it might be the Vietnam War, or it might be young people and drugs. Young people participate primarily because they see that there is a need. They recognise that something must be done, and they get up and do it. Participation brings about change.

Young people approach problems or issues with fresh eyes, and come up with simple solutions. Kuh's involvement in the Dance against Drugs is an example of an innovative approach to the issue of young people and drugs.

Young people may see things more clearly than adults may. Youth organisations in Rwanda tried to counteract the destruction of the civil war. The group of young people living with HIV who met in India in 1996 wanted to improve the quality of life for people living with HIV/AIDS. From the recognition of this need, there grew a powerful movement for change – the Indian Network for People Living with HIV.

- **A political will**

Young participants in civil society are not only socially aware, but they also enter into the political arena, recognising the power of politics to bring about change in civil society. Youth participation may mean opposition to or collaboration with government to bring about change.

Henry's school magazine spoke out against student government excesses. Later on Henry worked with the government, joining a national committee on Anti-AIDS

Strategy. Alphonsine represented young people at the Ministry of Youth and the Ministry of Education. Later, the youth organisations that Alphonsine belonged to tried to resolve ethnic divisions and civil war.

Even if a government is using young people in its own power struggle, young people are sometimes able to use this to their advantage. Edward recognised that the Dominican government invested in young people in the lead up to the election because they were a useful vote winner. Whatever the reasons behind the government's call for a National Youth Council, Edward assisted with its development because he recognised that the body had the potential to achieve young people's goals.

- **A lifetime commitment**

Perhaps the most important aspect of youth participation evident throughout these personal testimonies, is that the skills and the experience gained through youth participation last a lifetime. A person who is an active citizen at a young age is likely to remain an active citizen. The earlier a person develops decision making and participatory skills, the longer he or she has to develop those skills in the years following.

The recognition of a need for change lasts well beyond a person's youth. When a young person recognises that he or she has the power to change, that person will go on to change and influence society. Catherine Bertini's experiences as a young woman have directly impacted on her focus and on her priorities as an adult. It has no doubt influenced her career choices and her progress to becoming the Executive Director of a major UN agency.

All the youth activists featured in this chapter have acted as role models for new generations of young people. Ashok can inspire young people who have just discovered that they are HIV positive. Alphonsine's personal experiences give her more credibility and a greater identity with Girl Guides and Girl Scouts growing up in Africa today.

- **A voluntary commitment**

Youth participation is not financially rewarding. Indeed, more often than not a young person actually gives time and money to his or her activism. Youth participation has to therefore be a voluntary and altruistic commitment. All of the activists who have shared their personal pathways in this chapter have participated in civil society as volunteers. This has strengthened their motivation and had a positive impact on the shaping of their character.

Mainstreaming youth participation

Except in a few cases, youth participation always occurs within a youth-based environment, where the young person has joined a youth movement, or has established a youth organisation themselves.

In most cases, young people are not allowed to be part of a decision-making body, unless that body is part of a youth-based organisation. Even then, young people do not often get the chance to determine policy. Straight Talk is a young person's radio station. And so young people run it. But what about the policy-making body, the Straight Talk Foundation? The World Association of Girl Guides and Girl Scouts is very good at including young people at all levels of decision-making, but it is a youth-based organisation.

Real youth participation beyond youth organisations or beyond youth-led movements is a rare thing and certainly does not feature in the case studies in this chapter. Mainstream politics or the corporate sector rarely make a commitment to it.

Changing attitudes

Just like any activism, youth participation can sometimes be met with distrust and even persecution. Young people who rely on others for economic support may particularly feel this disapproval. Young people who join political debates, particularly those opposing the government, may face criticism from their families or from society. Young people like Kuh, who joined the recent demonstrations against the President, may be ostracised by their families.

Conclusion

These stories are all personal accounts written by exceptional people who actively chose to participate because they saw a need and because they had the right supportive and enabling environments. The key components of youth participation, identified as common threads through all of these personal pathways to empowerment, are:

- A personal commitment
- The influence of adults
- The influence of peers
- A need for change
- A political will
- A lifetime commitment
- A voluntary commitment

Chapter 5

The Challenge of Youth Citizenship:
From the Margins to the Centre

Kumi Naidoo

Introduction

As you read these words, several young people around the world will lose their lives – to AIDS, gun violence, the impact of environmental neglect or to landmines. Many will suffer, as social support systems and the criminal justice system fail young people. Others will suffer as a result of the failure of the so-called war on drugs, or will simply perish in various internal conflicts in countries around the world. Are young people, then, simply a problem that adults have to find solutions for?

On the contrary, despite all the challenges that young people face, it is they who provide the greatest innovation, have the greatest courage and put forth an amazing amount of voluntary energy and effort. Young people do not need to inhabit the fringes of public life, but can easily be in the centre. They are already beginning to occupy the centre in creative ways, even if it is to express their frustration or anger with their circumstances.

This book has made the argument that young people are not simply leaders of tomorrow, as is often said, but in very real ways are leaders of today. The experiences of individual youth leaders, as captured by Charlotte Baran in Chapter 3, and the examples of the efforts of youth organisations, as captured by Laila Duggan and Indira Ravindran in Chapter 4, suggest strongly that youth are on the move – with far greater skill, strategy and sense of purpose than ever before. Young people around the world are saying that they are not willing to be mere spectators on the sidelines, but that they want to be central players at different levels in the public sphere.

The participation of young people is nothing short of a demographic imperative. It has often been noted that young people, particularly in developing countries, are in the numeric majority. In some countries in Africa, for example, this is a growing tendency as the decimation caused by HIV/AIDS is reshaping the contours of the demographic map. The challenge faced by young people, as well as adult leaders of civil society organisations and their counterparts in business and government, is to create ways in which young people are treated as fully-fledged citizens. Young citizens have the right to be heard not only on the policy issues that confront various countries, but also policy choices facing global institutions such as the World Bank, the World Trade Organisation and the United Nations and its agencies. In short, advancing the agenda of youth participation may be no longer longer a nice thing to do, but it is a critical thing to achieve. In order to better explain this statement, I would like to disaggregate youth participation into three levels.

Levels of youth participation: macro, meso and micro

Macro: Young people want to address the fundamentals of governance, at the national and global levels.

Over the past few years, young people have increasingly begun to question the very essence of the public institutions that govern them. We are familiar with the phenomenon of students and youth activists taking to the streets in protest at unfair international trade agreements or corrupt, authoritarian governments. At a national level, even in long-standing democracies, young people are voicing their dissatisfaction as public institutions appear increasingly impotent, unpopular and unaccountable. Merely holding elections does not guarantee democratic participation and decision-making, and certainly does not enhance the role of young people in society. At a global level, young people have joined forces with experienced activists to raise fundamental questions about the governance of powerful global institutions such as the World Bank, International Monetary Fund (IMF) and the World Trade Organisation (WTO), and to propose alternatives. They are challenging inequitable political and economic structures, for example, the dangers of wealthier countries having disproportionate influence over international financial institutions. Another example is their questioning of the one dollar one vote system of the World Bank and the IMF at a time when world leaders have acknow -ledged that we need a new financial architecture that delivers greater equity and social justice.

Unconstrained by the 'that's just the way the world is' mentality, young people have the ability to pose questions in fresh ways that open the door to possibilities of fundamental institutional reform at the national and global levels.

Clearly, then, one important aspect of youth participation is the opening up of debates and exploration of alternatives to the institutional arrangements that the adult world takes as absolute and 'given', and beyond fundamental change and fundamental reform. Young people have inspired several adults to think with greater courage and vision in order to make substantive change that deals with issues of governance and power, and not just small administrative reforms. This does not negate the fact that many young people in urban and semi-urban areas around the world can often be apathetic, self-absorbed and with caught up with individualistic pursuits?

Meso: Young people want to engage with ongoing policy processes, and to influence outcomes to ensure that positive social and economic change continues.

Many young people, understandably, have reservations about the various flaws in the policy-making processes and the shape and form of public institutions at a national and global level. All the same, a significant number is committed to working for positive change within current constraints such as the youth-unfriendly governance of these institutions, youth voices not being taken seriously, and the gaps in accountability or 'democratic deficits' within institutions. At the national and provincial/statewide level young people, like many other socially excluded groups, find that the while the rules of participation is not in their favour. They find that it is critical to participate and try to influence the outcomes. Sometimes this is done to limit damage to policy positions, sometimes it is to advance a particular policy, and sometimes young people participate simply to better understand the rules of the institutions and processes with the view of developing a long-term strategy to change and challenge these rules. Given our working definition of young people as age thirty and under, we find that they are often present in a range of national policy processes where there are options for input and engagement by civil society organisations. On the down side, we find that often to be accepted in these processes they cannot advance a youth agenda too forcefully but have to subordinate this to other broader and more generic goals.

At a global level, young people are engaged to varying degrees and in a variety of ways with the diverse array of intergovernmental organisations and international processes. A growing number of international conferences have specific opportunities for young people to meet and develop their own positions on a range of issues. The work of a range of visionary thinkers in institutions such as the United Nations and the Commonwealth Secretariat who have consciously opened spaces for youth involvement, is salutary indeed. While some might say this is too little too late, it is still an important foundation that can be built upon and consolidated in coming years. Seeing young people as active and positive social agents, and not as victims, is not only the right thing to do but clearly the smart thing to do.

However, overall, there is a growing despondency in the ranks of many civil society leaders around the world as to whether engagement through dialogue with international institutions such as the UN, IMF, World Bank, WTO and so on, does actually yield substantive benefits. This despondency also rears its head within some youth organisations. Yet, many young leaders conclude that despite the limitations of these consultative processes, it is critical that they stay engaged with the current institutional framework to make the best of what is available .

Micro: Young people want to do real things for real people through a range of innovative programmatic interventions.

The number of young people participating directly in civil and political life via a diverse set of indigenous local and national youth organisations, is awe-inspiring.

The programmatic output of national and local youth organisations adds immense value to the overall social fabric in communities around the world. For example, the Chinese National Youth Foundation, is engaged in, amongst other things, youth leadership training as well as helping build schools in rural China. In Africa, various youth organisations are doing inspiring work around the HIV/AIDS pandemic.

Importantly, many youth-driven initiatives do not necessarily manifest themselves in formal youth organisations. Helping Hands Youth Organisation in Durban, South Africa, has been operating as a non-registered informal voluntary organisation since 1980, engaged in such diverse activities as civic and political education classes, education tuition in subjects such as Mathematics and Physics, coaching in swimming and athletics, and adopting various institutions offering care to abandoned children and those living with disabilities. In addition, gender awareness programmes and racial justice programmes also helped share information, develop skills, and build leadership. I was privileged to have been part of the leadership of Helping Hands. When I reflect on the work that I now do with CIVICUS and its affiliates, in promoting citizen participation and strengthening civil society, I have little doubt that most of what I know was learned in my years as a young activist.

Global youth movements and organisations such as the World Association of Girl Guides and Girl Scouts (WAGGGS), the International Youth Foundation (IYF), the World Organisation of the Scout Movement, the International Alliance of the YMCAs and YWCAs all offer great opportunities to youth to realise their potential. Chapter Three provides great personal examples of young people benefiting from such youth movements. Right now, many of these institutions are grappling with how to engage young people in the governance of their institutions, believing that including young people more effectively in decision-making can only enhance performance. The efforts of inter-governmental organisations such as the Commonwealth Secretariat and the UN also demonstrate healthy trends of youth participation in a range of initiatives around the world.

While issues of governance and management might still be at stake in many of these institutions, their global reach, the ability to develop inspiring leadership skills and build a community spiritedness, all combine to broaden and deepen youth participation.

Having examined the various levels of actual and potential youth participation in civil and political society, we must now consider the particular challenges and opportunities for youth participation. Here again, we must disaggregate our understanding of familiar concepts, including the most basic category of 'youth', so we may better understand the challenges and opportunities for youth participation.

Mapping out the Challenges and Opportunities for Youth Participation

Disaggregating youth: Guarding against homogenisation and respecting diversity

It is vital that in pursuing the objective of strengthening youth participation we do not treat young people as a monolith. Failure to understand the prevailing diversities could have disastrous consequences. What, then, are some of the key distinctions that need to be kept in mind? The first, and perhaps most important, is gender. Second, we have the distinctions that different age cohorts raise. Third, we need to be mindful of occupational locations: primary school, high or secondary schools, unemployed young people, professional young people, tertiary education and young workers. Fourth, cultural background and religion play identity-defining roles. Fifth, issues of race and ethnicity also need to be dealt with sensitively.

These diversities are not being brought up to suggest that young people cannot rise above such differences. In fact, young people are often better able to establish connections and unite across these boundaries, and have the ability to lead the way, for example, in fostering greater racial and ethnic justice and greater religious acceptance and tolerance. Failure to respect this diversity, on the other hand, could lead to programme failure and fail to harness the full potential of all young people.

Young people and globalisation

It is untrue that globalisation is fundamentally a new trend. The quest to connect across geographical divides predates the nation-state system as we know it today. Yet the scale of interaction is far greater today due to advances in the field of communications. Today, we find that young people have connected across national boundaries in creative ways, and that the flow of information has, in fact, fostered a virtual youth community that manifests itself in different ways across the world.

At the same time, we are confronted with the challenge of what Demos, a policy think tank in New York, has labelled 'economic apartheid'. Economic apartheid is also recognised as an important issue by UN ECLAC (Economic Commission for Latin America and the Caribbean), and the organisation's focus on 'equity, citizenship and development' is particularly refreshing.

Economic apartheid often has a distinct youth dimension, even though a small percentage of young people have benefited as a result of the Information Technology revolution. The sad reality, though, is that while some speed off on the information super-highway, millions more are left behind, stuck in their potholes, further debilitated by their lack of technical knowledge or the availability of infrastructure. As indicated in Chapter 4, the dominance of English on the internet also means that many other language groups are excluded.

On the positive side, information technology has played a pivotal role in broadening access to participation, while the sharing of experience has promoted cross-cultural learning and dialogue and has had an impact on how young people interact with each other and society as a whole. Notwithstanding the inequity in access to information and communications technology, known commonly as the 'digital divide', young people can be said to be participating, learning and leading in more creative, and often invisible ways. Just because you cannot see them does not mean they are not participating. The coming decades should see a greater intensification for those people who have technological access. This, unfortunately, means that those without access will be less involved in national or global processes, a challenge that we can only hope and work for, so that there is more equitable access, and more equitable and effective participation.

Young people and the social exclusion debate

In the coming decades, it would be a remarkable achievement indeed if humanity could judge itself not simply on the success of a few, but on the overall progress of everybody. In particular, humanity needs to rise to the challenge of addressing in creative, dynamic and courageous ways those who have been historically, and who continue to be, excluded from the mainstream of public life. In societies around the world, young people have been 'marginalised', seen as the 'lost generation' or 'Generation X' in search of self-identity, and as victims in need of salvation. Young people's alienation from public life is, in itself, a form of social exclusion that needs to be addressed. In a sense, this is the argument of all the preceding chapters in this book.

But more than that we also need to pose the question: how can young people, notwithstanding their own feelings of social exclusion, contribute to supporting the struggles for justice of other socially excluded groups? Being sensitive to questions of social exclusion also opens a powerful window into the work of other constituencies striving to create a more just world. This means that youth participation can be brought together with a poor community battling against environmental injustice, or finding the connections with many of the other socially excluded groups. The one caution here is that young people must ensure that when they interact with other constituencies, they work as partners, listen well, guard against framing people as victims, beneficiaries, recipients, clients or charity cases. It is critical that youth maintain the integrity of the people they seek to serve. In Africa, we have a proverb, 'I am because you are'. This is a powerful statement, which says that if you did not exist I would not exist. We acquire our identity, our sense of community, our meaning and purpose through our interaction with the other people in our lives. Therefore, when working with socially excluded groups, we need to be mindful that those of us who are 'serving' are in fact serving ourselves, since we often get so much more in return.

Young people and the challenge of leadership

Young people, as all the previous chapters have shown, are assuming important leadership roles all over the world. Young people's visibility in leadership is growing, not declining, and this needs to be consolidated, celebrated and expanded. The challenge however, is to recognise the multifaceted nature of youth leadership and ensure that there is always a conscious commitment to ensuring that leadership development is part of our work. Leadership development is a term that is frequently used in broad, sweeping terms, whereas in reality, it is very much context determined. From my position as a civil society practitioner, I see at least three distinct patterns of leadership development that are required in NGOs and other civil society organisations.

First, we have youth organisations constituted and led entirely by young people. Here, incumbent leaders need to ensure that they do not allow their own leadership, however inspiring and excellent, to prevent the rise of new leadership.

Second, we have the situation of young people working in youth organisations governed entirely, or mostly, by adults. In such organisations, there have been some positive movements in the right direction over the last ten years. Increasingly, young people are being brought into the governance structures of these institutions. For example, there has been a moderate rise in the number of young people being nominated to governing Boards of Directors . There is a also greater push to employ young people in the ranks of the administrative and programming staff of these organisations. These trends need to be strengthened.

Third, we have youth involvement in civil society organisations which do not focus exclusively on youth issues. Here again, the challenges are somewhat different. In fact, it is more difficult to develop youth leadership in these settings, since it is often suggested that the vision and mission, say of an economic or social justice movement, is so pressing that there is neither the time nor the resources to worry about youth leadership or other 'distracting' factors. Yet these organisations often rely on young people as their 'shock troops', 'foot soldiers' or 'work force'. These organisations must think deeply about how they relate to their youth constituency, and how they can ensure that their leadership role is not stunted, but is encouraged. Ultimately, the future vibrancy of many organisations depends on doing this effectively.

Youth organisations, and indeed all citizens' organisations, need to think constantly about nourishing youth leadership and fresh, innovative ideas. Therefore, youth organisations have to make investments in leadership development that are smart, courageous, innovative and cost-effective. This entails an investment in time and locally available resources, as well as the creation of conscious learning opportunities for young people, that take into account a full range of leadership skills. Fortunately, many innovative leadership programmes already exist; Chapter 4 features great examples. Such programmes need to be built upon, and incorporated as a natural part of the day-to-day life of these organisations.

Young people and the challenge of gender equality

The disproportionately low representation of young women in public life is truly scandalous. One must acknowledge the contributions of the women's movement around the world, which has opened up more spaces for active young women's leadership and has led to remarkable improvements in our approach to social issues over the past few decades. The UN Conference on Women held in Beijing in 1995 provided impetus to these developments, and several young women were inspired by the pre- and post-Beijing processes. Unfortunately, many youth organisations remain firmly dominated by young men and a range of societal norms hinder the participation of young women. The fact that young women carry a greater burden of responsibility for domestic work, for example, reduces the amount of time available for participation in public life, and in many societies young women are actively discouraged from seeking any avenues for public engagement.

Gender equality needs to be tackled at two levels by young people who believe that full democracy will never be achieved unless men and women share equitably in the democratic and economic process of their societies. The struggles for gender equality within youth organisations and in society as a whole have to be tackled simultaneously. Thankfully, more and more people, including a growing number of men, are saying that gender equality is central to creating a world that is environmentally sustainable, and in which social and economic justice reigns supreme. Given that even in long-standing democracies women still play a largely token part in establishment institutions, people need to ask themselves why are they willing to deprive societies of the vast experience, wisdom, sensitivity and creativity of more than half the world's population.

Young people, democracy and governance

Increasingly today, citizens around the world are arguing strongly that they want a greater involvement in public life than simply voting once every four or five years. The stale and old idea of 'governance being what government does' is being vigorously contested. Governance is being redefined as how policy decisions are made and what government and its citizens do, together and apart, to meet the needs of their societies. Many enlightened governments and international bodies increasingly seek out the voices of citizens' organisations and try to draw more people into the policy-making process. This is important at a time when, in fact, democracy is in a crisis. Fewer and fewer people are voting and electoral systems are becoming less and less accessible to ordinary people. There is diminishing internal democracy, transparency and openness within powerful political parties, even in countries with long-standing histories of party politics. There is a growing sense that national governments in poor countries are powerless in the face of influential global institutions. We see that formal electoral democracy is unable to deliver economic justice in many parts of the world. All these realities have combined to create a huge distance between elected officials and their citizens.

What, then, are the specific challenges for young people? The most important challenge is to ensure that young people do not slide into cynicism, but continue to remain critically engaged with democratic institutions, however flawed. Young people of voting age should vote, even if it is only to 'spoil' or invalidate their ballots if there are no candidates worth voting for, as a sign of protest at the choices available to them. Apathy should be challenged. The time has also come for a serious reconsideration of the voting age. Today, young people often have as much or more access to information as their parents do. Young people have important responsibilities and, hence, they should be more involved in democratic processes and public life. For some time now, some of us have been calling for the voting age limit to be reduced to 16. It is worth bearing in mind that President Nelson Mandela, in acknowledgement of the role young school students played in the struggle against apartheid, once called for 14-year-olds to be given the vote.

As suggested by Steve Mokwena in Chapter 2, young people have a big role to play in addressing the democratic deficit at various formal and informal institutional levels. Young people have played a central role historically in struggles for democracy around the world and this continues today. There are many youth heroes who have given their lives to see democracy prevail. In meeting the challenges for greater democracy in the world, young people need to operate at three levels. At the macro level, we need to be looking at what substantive changes need to be made in the rules, procedures and laws that guide our lives at a local, national and global level. Perhaps it is going to take the imagination and the creativity of young people to think more courageously and innovatively about what changes need to be made so that our public institutions are the best they can be to meet all of humanity's needs.

At a meso level, while recognising that institutional change is a marathon and not a sprint, we still need to ensure that we try to make the current processes work as well as possible. How can we get more young people running for public office, voting, campaigning and shaping the election agenda? At a global level, how can we ensure, for example, that the forthcoming UN conferences, such as the conference on the environment and sustainable development (Earth Summit 2002), to be held in Johannesburg, has a strong youth voice and presence? Young people and those not yet born are, perhaps, the most important stakeholders in the environment.

At a micro level, young people should be engaged in specific projects around voter education, civic education, promoting adult literacy and so on. All three levels of participation are important and it is incumbent upon young people to establish links between these levels.

Youth participation in developing a new world vision

We should resist the idea that the world is largely fine and there are a few minor problems that need to be addressed. Indeed we should celebrate humanity's considerable achievements but we should not allow complacency to set in or allow a very low threshold of expectations about what our world could be. Surely, when there is so much affluence and wealth in the world but we are unable to prevent homelessness, hunger, starvation, disease and conflict, then something is not working and we must believe that there is a solution to be pursued and found. Young people have the advantage that they are not overly burdened by too much of the cynicism and practices of the adult world. They are probably better able to imagine a world where there is no homelessness or war, and one in which justice prevails. So one of the roles that young people should engage in is visionary scenario planning. Getting young people to think about the future and about what new paradigms might work is an important avenue to pursue. But this need not just be a long-term, romantic enterprise. Young people can and should be looking at creative and new ways for organisations to operate and rethink their strategies.

I can provide two examples of novel ways in which young people have 'broken the mould'. Rather than view the relationship between corporations and civil society organisations as primarily adversarial or merely a one-time flirtation captured by a donation or grant, young people have participated in encouraging civil society organisations and businesses to creatively seek common ground, and work out ways of channelling the considerable resources of the latter towards social development. For many civil society organisations, this approach of exploring common ground with business required them to 'think out of the box'. Of course, finding the appropriate terms of these inter-relationships is always difficult, but there is evidence that more people in need can be reached and supported by such partnerships. CIVICUS has published a pioneering study called 'Promoting Corporate Citizenship: Opportunities for Business and Civil Society Engagement' outlining the challenges, possibilities and opportunities to move the relationship between NGOs and the business community beyond donations and funding grants to harnessing business's full resources.

Another example of 'breaking the mould' has to do with how we think about issues of gender equality generally, and an issue like violence against women and children in particular. In the past, violence against women was treated as a woman's issue, to be taken up by women's organisations. In reality, as some men have repeatedly pointed out, this is fundamentally a men's issue. It is men who are the perpetrators and the problem is rooted in how masculinity is constructed and understood. So education and outreach efforts should target men as well as women. Rethinking some of our fundamental conceptual frames and some of the ways in which we work, and linking that to more substantive issues can create a more just and equitable world. In meeting this challenge, young people have an indispensable role.

From mazes to GRACES: integrating youth work with broader social and economic change

Sometimes, the youth participation agenda is unable to move forward and is trapped in a maze of intrigue because it does not actively intersect with the range of other social interventions that are underway. We can move out of this maze of isolation if we embrace the intersectionality of youth participation and youth citizenship with some key areas of voluntary action for positive social and economic change. Inspired by those women activists who have refused to be parochial in vision and have made common cause with other citizen movements that work for social and economic change, I propose GRACES* as a simpler way to talk about the challenge of intersectionality. GRACES: G stands for full gender equality and raises the question of what special actions are needed to ensure the full participation of young women in public life. R raises the question of how we can work for racial justice and religious tolerance. A deals with age and ability, C deals with class, community and caste, E deals with ethnicity and S covers those that are otherwise socially excluded, such as people living with HIV/AIDS or other illnesses and disabilities, indigenous people and those who face discrimination because of their sexual orientation.

Conclusion

Advancing the agenda of active youth citizenship will, of course, not be served by romanticising youth participation. While we look at the abundant benefits, opportunities and energies that can be harnessed to breathe new energy into what has become stale, moribund and tired public life, we need also to note the limitations that understandably hold back youth participation. However, in examining such limitations, adult public figures, especially, should recognise that each generation brings with it certain objective limitations. These limitations should not be read as something that should limit our exploration of making youth citizenship real and active, but should be understood just as another general challenge that needs to be met with creativity and realism.

Any agenda to harness the full participation of youth in public life should take as its starting point the need to develop and build appropriate generational linkages. This is a matter of priority, considering that the growing sense of alienation experienced by young people is linked to serious generational cleavages that fail to make use of inter-generational synergy. The need for this sort of prioritisation is illustrated by the work of the Global Meeting of Generations, a civil society organisation which seeks to bring together the wisdom of multiple generations in framing a new approach to sustainable development.

Young people need to feel enabled to take initiatives to deal with the challenges that they face. Just as importantly, youth leaders and adults should encourage young people to be major societal stakeholders; stakeholders who have the ability to offer creative contributions to the challenges facing humanity as a whole. Failure to do so will squander the great potential that active youth participation can offer to the world.

---

*'GRACES' was inspired by comments made by participants at the founding meeting of the 'Gender at Work Collaborative' convened by UNIFEM, CIVICUS, Women's Learning Partnership and the Association for Women's Rights in Development in June 2001.

Further Reading on Youth Participation

Under each heading, articles in journals follow stand-alone publications.

General

14 points: successfully involving youth in decision making. Available for order online at: www.youthonboard.org

Slayton, Elaine Doremus, *Empowering Teens: A Guide to Developing a Community Based Youth Organization.*

Youth participation manual/Economic and Social Commission for Asia and the Pacific. New York: United Nations, 2000. United Nations publication, Sales No. E.00.II.F.43. T.p. verso. Includes bibliographical references, pp. 43–44.

Reason, Peter and Bradbury, Hilary, eds. *Handbook of action research: participative inquiry and practice.* London; Thousand Oaks, Calif.: SAGE, 2001. See especially: Reason and Bradbury, 'Introduction'; Heron and Reason, '16. The Practice of Co-operative Inquiry'; Senge and Scharmer, '22. Community Action Research'; Bhatt and Tandon, '28. Citizen Participation in Natural Resource Management'; Kelly, Mock and Tandon, '34. Collaborative Inquiry with African American Community Leaders'; Whitmore and McKee, '40. Six Street Youth Who Could ... '. ISBN 0 76196 645 5

Smith, Mark, *Developing youth work: informal education, mutual aid, and popular practice.* Milton Keynes, Bucks; Philadelphia: Open University Press, 1988. ISBN/ISSN 0 33515 835 8: ISBN/ISSN 0 33515 834 X (pbk.). Youth and community work in the 70s: proposals. Great Britain. Youth Service Development Council. London: HM Stationery Office, 1969.

Keeble, R.W.J., *A life full of meaning: some suggestions and some material for the future training of youth leaders.* Oxford; New York: Pergamon Press, 1965.

Hahn, A., *Quantum Opportunities Program: A Brief on the QOP Pilot Program.* Waltham, MA: Brandeis University, Heller School, Center for Human Resources, 1995.

Hahn, A., *Evaluation of the Quantum Opportunities Program (QOP): Did the Program Work?* Waltham, MA: Brandeis University, Heller School, Center for Human Resources, 1994.

Forster, Peter G. and Nsibande, Bongani S. (eds), *Swaziland: contemporary social and economic issues.* Aldershot: Ashgate, 2000. See Part II, Philip F. Iya, '4. Meeting the Needs of Youth in National Development Policy and Its Legal Implications in Swaziland'; Part III, Thandi F. Khumalo, '8. Community Participation in Urban Planning and Development'. ISBN 1 84014 331 2

Cooke, Bill and Kothari, Uma (eds), *Participation: the new tyranny?* London; New York: Zed Books, 2001. See Nicholas Hildyard, Pandurang Hegde and Paul Wolvekamp, '4. Pluralism, Participation and Power: Joint Forest Management in India'; Giles Mohan, '10. Beyond Participation: Strategies for Deeper Empowerment'. ISBN 1 85649 793 3 (cased); 1 85649 794 1 (limp).

Naul, F.M. and C.E., *Targeting youth: Empirical evidence, conceptual issues and rationales.* Washington, DC. Paper prepared for the World Bank, Human Resources Division, Country Department III, Latin America and the Caribbean Region, 1996.

Ewen, John, 'Youth participation: Concepts and structures', *Youth Studies*, Spring 1994, Vol. 13, Issue 3.

'Australia's movement towards youth participation from the 1960s to the present'. AN: 9501125219; ISSN: 0818–7886T.

Kirkman, Bradley L. and Rosen, Benson. 'Powering Up Teams', *Organizational Dynamics*, Winter 2000, Vol. 28, Issue 3; pp. 48; 18p, 1 diagram. How some organisations are getting more from work teams by empowering them. Distinction between empowered teams and self-managing teams.

Randolph, W. Alan. 'Navigating the journey to empowerment'. *Organizational Dynamics*, Spring 1995, Vol. 23, Issue 4. Observes several companies that successfully made a shift from a bureaucracy to an empowering management.

Activism and leadership

The Kenya National Youth Service: a governmental response to young political activists. Athens, Ohio: Ohio University, Center for International Studies, 1973.

Close, Carole L. and Lechman, Kathy. 'Fostering youth leadership', *Theory into Practice*, Winter 1997, Vol. 36, Issue 1; pp. 11; 6p. Focuses on a programme which is being set up to educate adults and students on how to handle conflict resolution.

Des Marais, Joy, Yang, Youa and Farzanehkia, Farid. 'Service-Learning Leadership Development for Youths', *Phi Delta Kappan*, May 2000, Vol. 81, Issue 9; pp. 678; 3p, 1bw. Argues that the goals of service-learning must include the development of leadership skills in students. AN: 3078348; ISSN: 0031–7217T

Hillcoat, John and Forge, Karen, '"I think it's really great that someone is listening to us ...": Young people and the environment', *Environmental Education Research*, 1995, Vol. 1, Issue 2; pp. 159; 13p.

'Outside the fence: Young activists inspired despite violent protests at Quebec summit', Canadian Press, 21 April 2001

Weaver II, Richard L., 'Motivating the motivators: Eight characteristics for empowering those who empower others', *Executive Speeches*, August/September 1996, Vol. 11, Issue 1; pp. 35; 3p. Speech by communications professor Richard L. Weaver II on employee motivation in the USA. Requisites of credibility; importance of sociability, optimism, competence and extroversion; development of character.

Citizenship/political education

Hahn, Carole L., 'What Can Be Done to Encourage Civic Engagement in Youth?', *Social Education*, March 2001, Vol. 65, Issue 2; pp. 108; 3p, 1c. Highlights the findings of research conducted in five democratic countries concerning citizenship education.

Hall, Tom and Coffey, Amanda. 'Self, Space and Place: youth identities and citizenship', *British Journal of Sociology of Education*, December 1999, Vol. 20, Issue 4; pp. 501; 13p. Identity, citizenship and social change as experienced by young people in the UK. Debates about citizenship in the UK currently encompass a range of themes which go beyond an understanding of citizenship as a simply technical or legal term.

Maoz, Ifat, 'An Experiment in Peace: Reconciliation-Aimed Workshops of Jewish-Israeli and Palestinian Youth', *Journal of Peace Research*, 11/1/00, Vol. 37. No. 6; pp. 721–36. Examines workshops of Jewish-Israeli and Palestinian youth organised by an Israeli-Palestinian organisation in the post-Oslo era.

McEvoy, Siobhán, 'Communities and Peace: Catholic Youth in Northern Ireland', *Journal of Peace Research*, 1/1/00, Vol. 37, No. 1; pp. 85–103. Focuses on young people between the ages of 13 and 18 years in the wake of the Good Friday Agreement of 1998. Perceptions of their own roles in peacebuilding; how it is hampered by the institutionalised bipolarity of the political system and by a system of communal deterrence.

Morrison, A., 'Introduction: Education for liberation', *Social Policy*, Winter 1991, Vol. 21, Issue 3; pp. 2; 4p. Profiles the Highlander Folk School, Tennessee, founded in 1932 as a centre for democratic education and political activism. Empowering oppressed people in the heart of Appalachia; fighting class, race, and gender domination.

Pring, Richard, 'Political Education: relevance of the humanities', *Oxford Review of Education*, March–June 1999, Vol. 25, Issue 1/2; pp. 71; 17p. Discusses the tradition of political education that is rooted in the teaching of the humanities. Details on the political understanding of education, or the relationship of power and authority between government, teacher, parent and pupil.

Watts, Meredith W., 'Orientations toward conventional and unconventional ...', *Comparative Political Studies*, October 1990, Vol. 23, Issue 3; pp. 283; 31p, 5 charts. Politics among adolescents and young adults in West Germany. Politicalisation of young people; extent to which youth is internally differentiated in its political development.

West, Jackie, '(Not) talking about sex: Youth, identity and sexuality', *Sociological Review*, August 1999, Vol. 47, Issue 3; pp. 525; 23p, Social constraints on young people's opportunities for talk and discussion about sex, with reference to their experiences of sex education and services in sexual health. Limited social acceptance of teenage sexuality and the forms of its regulation; how questions of sexual citizenship are closely connected to wider issues of social equality.

Community development

Daniels, Mark R. (ed.), *Creating sustainable community programs: examples of collaborative public administration*. Westport, Conn.: Praeger, 2001. See Alice E. Kaiser-Drobney, 'Chapter 18. Engaging Youth in Their Communities'. ISBN 0275967743 (alk. paper).

Mullahey, Ramona, Susskind, Yve and Checkoway, Barry, *Youth participation in community planning*. Chicago, Ill.: American Planning Association, 1999.

Rauner, Diana Mendley, *They still pick me up when I fall: the role of caring in youth development and community life*. New York: Columbia University Press, 2000. ISBN/ISSN 0 23111 854 6 (cl); ISBN/ISSN 0 23111 855 4 (pa).

Batavick, Laney, 'Community-based family support and youth development: Two movements, one philosophy', *Child Welfare*, September/October 1997, Vol. 76, Issue 5; pp. 639; 25p, 1 chart. Examines the key elements and the relative success of family support and youth development practice. Suggestions for integrating youth development and family support programmes.

Finn, Janet L and Checkoway, Barry, 'Young people as competent community builders', *Social Work*, July 1998, Vol. 43, Issue 4; pp. 335; 11p. Covers a pilot study conducted on an exemplary community-based initiative in the USA.

Manandhar, Udaya and Leslie, Keith, 'Empowering women and families through literacy in Nepal', *Convergence*, 1994, Vol. 27, Issue 2–3; pp. 102; 9p.

McLaughlin, Milbrey W., 'Community Counts', *Educational Leadership*, April 2001, Vol. 58, Issue 7; pp. 14; 5p, 2c, 1bw. Focuses on an investigation of participation of young students in community-based programmes in the USA. Types of community organisations preferred by young people; benefits of programme participation to students; actions that can be done by schools to support community youth organisations.

Parker, Lenore M. and Franco, Maria L., 'Empowering Youths to Build Community through Service', *Social Work in Education*, July 1999, Vol. 21, Issue 3; pp. 163; 13p, 4 charts. Focuses on young people's attitudes toward service and extent of service activities.

Simpson, Brian, 'Towards the participation of children and young people in urban planning and design', *Urban Studies*, May 1997, Vol. 34, Issue 5/6; pp. 907; 19p.

Travers, Robb and Paoletti, Dino, 'The lesbian, gay & bisexual youth programme (LGBYP): A model for communities seeking to improve quality of life for lesbian, gay and bisexual youth', *Canadian Journal of Human Sexuality*, 1999, Vol. 8, Issue 4; pp. 293; 11p.

Marginalised young people

Brendtro, Larry K., Brokenleg, Martin and Van Bockern, Steve, *Reclaiming youth at risk: our hope for the future*. Bloomington, Ind.: National Educational Service, 1998. ISBN/ISSN 1 87963 905 X.

Harrell, A. V. with Burt, M. R., Hatry, H., Rossman, S., Roth, J. and Sabol, W., *Evaluating programmes for vulnerable children and youth.* Washington, DC. Paper prepared for the World Bank, Human Resources Division, Country Department III, Latin America and the Caribbean Region, 1995b.

Heath, Shirley Brice and McLaughlin, Milbrey W. (eds), *Identity and inner-city youth: beyond ethnicity and gender*. New York: Teachers College Press, 1993.

Brendtro, Larry K., Ness, Arlin and colleagues, *Re-educating troubled youth: environments for teaching and treatment*. New York: Aldine Publishing Co., c.1983. ISBN/ISSN 0 20236 033 4; ISBN/ISSN 0 20236 034 2 (pbk).

McIntyre, Alice, *Inner-city kids: adolescents confront life and violence in an urban community*. New York: New York University Press, 2000. Qualitative studies in psychology series. ISBN/ISSN 0 81475 635 2 (cl:alk.paper); ISBN/ISSN 0 81475 636 0 (pbk).

Barker, G. and Fuentes, M., *Review and Analysis of International Experience with programmes Targeted on at-Risk Youth*. Washington, DC: Paper prepared for the World Bank, Human Resources Division, Country Department III, Latin America and the Caribbean Region, 1995.

Dwyer, Peter, *Opting out: Early school leavers and the degeneration of youth policy*. Hobart: National Clearinghouse for Youth Studies, 1996, 88pp. ISBN 1 87523 634 1. This Youth Research Centre report determines the concerns, problems and needs of those defined as early leavers, and identifies effective strategies that would give them the opportunity to choose to continue their schooling beyond the compulsory years.

Resnick, G., Burt, M.R., Newmark, L. and Reilly, L., *Youth at Risk: Definitions, Prevalence, and Approaches to Service Delivery*. Washington, DC: Urban Institute, 1992.

Abery, Brian and Simunds, Erin, 'The Yes I Can Social Inclusion Program: A preventive approach to challenging behavior', *Intervention in School & Clinic*, March 1997, Vol. 32, Issue 4; pp.223, 12p. Includes discussion of social inclusion of students and socially isolated young adults with disabilities.

Brown, Chris, 'Marginalised young people and the power of decision making', *Youth Studies*, November 1991, Vol. 10, Issue 4; pp,41; 6p, 1bw. Looks at the capacity of human service organisations to address the marginalisation experienced by young people.

Farmer, Lesley, 'Empowering young women through information literacy', *Emergency Librarian*, May/June 1996, Vol. 23, Issue 5; pp.17; 4p. Role of teacher-librarians.

Fleming, J. and Keenan, E., 'Youth on the margins in Northern Ireland, England, and Ukraine', *Nutritional Neuroscience* 7 January 2000, Vol 3, No. 2; pp.165–77. Perspectives on the situation of young people, with examples of blocks to the inclusion of young people in their societies. Marginalisation is a topical concept in all three places with elements that transcend cultural and national boundaries.

Kern-Foxworth, Marilyn, 'Growing Our Own', *Black Issues in Higher Education*, 10 December 2000, Vol. 17, Issue17; pp.50; 1p. Importance of assisting Afro-Americans to decision-making power. Role of national organisations in improving potentials; need for programmes that allow young people set their goals.

Nagorski, Maria, 'Volunteer program empowers youths', *Corrections Today*, August 1996, Vol. 58, Issue 5; pp.171; 2p. Focuses on the Youth as Resources (YAR) program of the Indiana Department of Corrections which provides juvenile delinquents with sense of belonging, self-worth, responsibility and community connection.

Urban Institute, *Nurturing young black males: Programs that work*. Washington, DC: Urban Institute, 1995.

Health

Caputo, Tullio, *Hearing the voices of youth: youth participation in selected Canadian municipalities*. Ottawa: Health Canada, 2000. Also in French.

Winter, Micha de, *Children as fellow citizens: participation and commitment*. Oxford: Radcliffe Medical Press, 1997.

Harper, Gary W. and Carver, Lisa J., '"Out-of-the-Mainstream" Youth as Partners in Collaborative Research: Exploring the Benefits and Challenges', *Health Education & Behavior*, April 1999, Vol. 26, Issue 2; pp.250; 16 pp. Describes a successful university community-based organisation collaboration that was formed to explore HIV-related risk rates and prevention strategies for suburban street youth. Criteria used to select the youth hired into the project; conclusions. AN: 1683007; ISSN: 1090–1981T

Holland, J. and Ramazanoglu, C., 'Risk, power and the possibility of pleasure', *AIDS Care*, 1992, Vol. 4, Issue 3; pp. 273; 11p. Prevention of HIV in young women highlighting aspect of safe sexual practices. Reference to research initiated by the Women Risk and AIDS Project (WRAP); details of the WRAP project.

Laveman, Larry, 'The Harmonium Project: A Macrosystemic Approach to Empowering Adolescents', *Journal of Mental Health Counseling*, January 2000, Vol. 22, Issue 1; pp. 17; 15p. Covers a community-based agency that conducts collaborative, strength-based counselling. Problems at home, school or in the community viewed in an integrated manner.

WHO/UNFPA/UNICEF Study Group on Programming for Adolescent Health, 1995. Programming for Adolescent Health: Discussion Paper, November 28–December 4, 1995. Saillon, Switzerland.

Education

Banks, James A., *Cultural diversity and education: foundations, curriculum, and teaching*. Boston; London: Allyn & Bacon, 2001. 4th ed. See Part 4, 'Curriculum and Teaching Strategies'; 10. 'A Curriculum for Empowerment, Action, and Change'; 11. 'Teaching Decision Making and Social Action Skills'. ISBN 0 20530 865 1

Gomez de Souza, Luis A. and Ribeiro, Lucia, *Youth participation in the development process: a case study in Panama*, International Educational Reporting Service. Experiments and innovations in education, No. 18. Paris: Unesco Press, 1976.

Chopra, Raj K, 'Using technology in schools to empower our young people', *NASSP Bulletin*, September 1994, Vol. 78, Issue 563; p1, 9p. Integration of technology into the Shawnee Mission, Kansas. Selection of pilot schools; success factors.

Dryfoos, J., *Full service schools: A revolution in health and social services for children, youth and families*. Experiments and innovations in education, no. 18. San Francisco: Jossey-Bass Publishers, 1994.

Frankham, Jo. 'Peer education: The unauthorised version', *British Educational Research Journal*, April 1998, Vol. 24, Issue 2; pp. 179, 15p. Highlights the increase in use of peer education in the UK.

Fraser, James W, 'Preparing teachers for democratic schools: The Holmes and Carnegie reports five years later ...', *Teachers College Record*, Fall 1992, Vol. 94, Issue 1; p7; 34p. What the reports contained; the need for an arts and sciences major; why recruit minorities into the teaching profession; more.

Kubow, Patricia K, 'Fostering Democracy in Middle School Classrooms: Insights from a Democratic Institute in Hungary', *Social Studies*, November/December 2000, Vol. 91, Issue 6; pp. 265; 7p. Concepts, application and results of democratic classroom practice.

Contributors

Charlotte Barran is Head of Communications for the World Association of Girl Guides and Girl Scouts (WAGGGS) which is based in London. She is responsible for WAGGGS' external relations. She works closely with the UN and with international NGOs and IGOs on issues affecting girls and young women throughout the world. Charlotte, 28, graduated from the University of Edinburgh in 1996 where she studied English and Philosophy.

Laila Duggan worked as an intern for CIVICUS 2000–2001 on a Canadian government funded programme. She was based at the CYP Asia Regional Centre in Chandigarh, India. The focus of her work was communications and networking with NGOs in the Commonwealth Asia region. Laila undertook the daunting task of identification, liaison collecting and collating of case studies from contributors. Laila has returned to Vancouver, Canada to continue her career in communications.

Jane Foster is Head of the Commonwealth Youth Programme. She has worked in youth empowerment work for over twenty years. Her experience encompasses policy development in international youth affairs, management in local government, and teaching and training in many settings, from tertiary institutions to the non-formal sector. A New Zealander, she has worked in New Zealand, the UK, the South Pacific and across the Commonwealth.

Steve Mokwena is a leading youth development advocate – programmer-practitioner – and writer from South Africa. Steve served as the Chief Executive Officer of the National Youth Commission in the Office of the Deputy President in South Africa. Before taking full-time employment, he was involved with student, political and grassroots youth organizations. Steve has written and published papers on youth development, youth culture and youth policy. Later he managed cross-sectoral and multi-country projects on Youth and Community Development for IYF/Ford Foundation International Learning Group involving researchers from Asia, Latin America, Europe and Africa. Steve was educated in South Africa and the UK.

Kumi Naidoo is Secretary General and Chief Executive Officer of CIVICUS: World Alliance for Citizens Participation. He was the founding executive director of the South African NGO Coalition (SANGOCO) and served in leadership positions in the adult education NGO sector in South Africa. Kumi played an active role in student and youth associations during the 1980s and spent two years as volunteer house-father/counsellor for adolescent boys. He was expelled from school in South Africa at the age of 15 as a result of his anti-apartheid activities. He is a Rhodes Scholar and holds degrees in Politics and Law, including a Doctorate in Political Sociology from Oxford University.

Indira Ravindran works as Communications and Research Associate at CIVICUS. As an undergraduate in India, she was active in the National Service Scheme (NSS), a nation-wide, government-supported programme that promotes youth volunteerism. Through the NSS, Indira had the opportunity to work with homeless and intellectually challenged children, as well as participate in an adult literacy programme. As a graduate student in the USA, she has been involved in various campaigns for social justice conducted at the local and transnational levels. Indira is pursuing a PhD in Political Science (focus on postcolonial studies) at the Johns Hopkins University, USA.